Getting Data Science Done

Getting Data Science Done

Managing Projects From Ideas to Products

John Hawkins

BUSINESS EXPERT PRESS
Leader in applied, concise business books

First published in 2022 by
Business Expert Press, LLC
222 East 46th Street, New York, NY 10017
www.businessexpertpress.com

ISBN-13: 978-1-63742-277-9 (paperback)
ISBN-13: 978-1-63742-278-6 (e-book)

Business Expert Press Big Data, Business Analytics, and Smart Technology Collection

First edition: 2022

10 9 8 7 6 5 4 3 2 1

Description

Data science is a field that synthesizes statistics, computer science and business analytics to deliver results that can impact almost any type of process or organization. Data science is also an evolving technical discipline, whose practice is full of pitfalls and potential problems for managers, stakeholders and practitioners. Many organizations struggle to consistently deliver results with data science due to a wide range of issues, including knowledge barriers, problem framing, organizational change and integration with IT and engineering.

Getting Data Science Done outlines the essential stages in running successful data science projects. The book provides comprehensive guidelines to help you identify potential issues and then a range of strategies for mitigating them. The book is organized as a sequential process allowing the reader to work their way through a project from an initial idea all the way to a deployed and integrated product.

Keywords

learn data science; data science process; managing data science projects; problem framing; project management; predictive analytics; machine learning delivery; data science solutions

Contents

Preface

This book began in 2014 as a collection of notes I was taking on the general process of running a data science project. It was largely driven by a desire to improve my own process and bring more discipline to how I delivered results. It was also inspired by my personal curiosity about the extent to which data science can be distilled into a procedure that can be automated.

If you spend any time with data scientists, you will soon discover that one of their favorite topics for lunchtime conversations is whether their job can be automated. This is the data scientist's existential dilemma. We are, to a large extent, involved in the process of reshaping jobs and automating many tasks. It is therefore natural to ponder whether our jobs will suffer the same fate.

As I worked on this book and read more about data science project delivery, it became clearer to me that the predominant reasons that data science projects fail are not technical. Projects either never get to the stage where a technical solution can be built or the solution is never taken through to production because it solved the wrong problem. These failures are less about the technical decisions involved, and more about how data scientists nurture the stakeholders of the project.

Consequently, this book is different from most data science books. It is about how you effectively deliver data science projects from the first meeting to the last. To this end, my focus is on the aspects of data science that are not covered by other books. Some of these topics are semitechnical, including the choice of metrics and interventions, but many would be more accurately classified as soft skills. This includes framing a problem and recognizing the real problem that needs to be solved (as opposed to what your client or manager is asking of you), and many other skills related to managing and delivering an analytics project. Some of these skills are common to running any kind of technical project, but because of the unusual nature of data science they take on their own flavor.

This can include project scoping, expectation setting, communication, prioritization, documentation, and project management.

All these aspects of a data science project are necessary, but generally receive little to no attention in data science courses. The lack of development of these topics means that as a community we tend to do these things poorly. Everything in this book I have either learned the hard way or learned from watching and working with people who are much better at these things than I am.

It has been my experience that far too many projects fail for preventable reasons that have little to do with the technical capability of the data scientists involved. I hope that you find the ideas collected herein useful in driving your own projects, and I hope you will not hesitate to reach out and let me know how they work for you.

Acknowledgments

This book would not have been possible without the numerous fantastic colleagues I have worked with over the years. People from whom I have learned through collaboration and argument, as well as observation of success and failure. In particular, my former academic supervisors William Herfel and Mikael Bodén, both of whom exerted a great deal of influence on the development of my thought patterns. My former colleagues David Rowe, Jesse Wu, Sabrina Rodrigues, and James Petterson with whom I have discussed many of the specific ideas and problems in this book.

I am immensely grateful to David Dufty, Sabrina Rodrigues, Jesse Wu, Trung Nguyen, Will Hanninger, and Gourab De for reviewing and providing invaluable feedback on this manuscript. I would like to thank Scott Isenberg from BEP for his guidance on preparing and publishing this book. I am grateful to my wife Diamond Hawkins for supporting me through the process, and finally, to my mother Margaret Hawkins for allowing me the intellectual freedom to discover what I loved doing.

Introduction

Data science projects regularly fail to deliver results. Industry analysts report a spread of statistics, with conservative estimates suggesting that projects completely fail, or result in insufficient returns, almost as often as they succeed.[1] More pessimistic estimates put failure as the dominant outcome.[2] When executives are surveyed on their understanding of these issues, technology is not seen as the source of the problem. Instead, it is recognized that people and processes are impeding the ability of organizations to implement big data or analytics solutions.[3]

Investigations into specific failures reveal a variety of contributing factors. It can be a combination of organizational change challenges, poor problem framing, issues with data quality, and an inability to productionize results. More importantly, for practitioners of data science, it has been identified that many machine learning and analytics experts are not spending enough time and energy on defining the right problem, and then driving toward a specific business outcome.[4] Instead, they focus on further development of downstream technical solutions that, counterintuitively, provide relatively low value.[5]

---

[1] S. Ransbotham, S. Khodabandeh, R. Fehling, B. Lafountain, and D. Kiron. October 15, 2019. "Winning with AI," *Sloan Management Review*. https://sloanreview .mit.edu/projects/winning-with-ai/

[2] Dimensional Research. May 2019. "Artificial Intelligence and Machine Learning Projects Are Obstructed by Data Issues," *Whitepaper*, (downloaded, August 2021), https://content.alegion.com/dimensional-researchs-survey

[3] R. Bean and T.H. Davenport. February 05, 2019. "Companies Are Failing in Their Efforts to Become Data-Driven," *Harvard Business Review*. https://hbr .org/2019/02/companies-are-failing-in-their-efforts-to-become-data-driven

[4] M. Ross and B.G.S. Hardie. July–August 2021. "Why You Aren't Getting More from Your Marketing AI," *Harvard Business Review*. https://hbr.org/2021/07/ why-you-arent-getting-more-from-your-marketing-ai

[5] K. Veeramachaneni. December 07, 2016. "Why You're Not Getting Value from Your Data Science," *Harvard Business Review*. https://hbr.org/2016/12/why-youre-not-getting-value-from-your-data-science

When we turn to what is written about these problems by data science consultants and analytics software vendors, we see a similar pattern. Explanations of failure tend to fall into one of two different categories: those that have to do with misunderstandings about what data science can do and poor specification of the problem statements;[6] and those related to resources, either inadequate data or access to teams of people with the right skill sets.[7]

In the following chapters, we will be exploring the ways these problems manifest themselves throughout the project life cycle. I will discuss strategies for mitigating the problems where possible, and approaches for identifying and managing risks in other situations. By discussing these issues in an approximately sequential fashion, my hope is that it will help you get an understanding of how unresolved issues early in a project can manifest themselves later as much larger problems.

---

[6] R. Harrington. March 22, 2019. "Why Do Machine Learning Projects Fail?" *CompassRed Data Blog.* https://medium.com/compassred-data-blog/why-do-machine-learning-projects-fail-9d9ec514b2ab; **B.** Ito. April 01, 2019. "7 Ways Machine Learning Projects Fail," Retina AI Blog. https://retina.ai/blog/7-ways-machine-learning-projects-fail/

[7] B. Dickson. February 25, 2021. "Why Most Machine Learning Strategies Fail," *TechTalks Blog.* https://bdtechtalks.com/2021/02/25/machine-learning-strategy-barriers/

PART I
Problem Framing

CHAPTER 1

Getting Started

A problem well stated is a problem half solved.

—Charles Kettering

At the start of any project, there is a period when everyone involved is trying to determine what the project means for them. The resulting project scope will include a definition of what is being delivered, who is delivering it, and the arrangement of milestones across the timeline. In data science work, there is usually an additional stage at the beginning. Before any of the specific deliverables can be defined, you will need to analyze and understand the problem you are solving.

The problems that are solved with data science work are many and varied. However, they are all typically not the kind of thing that can be solved by simply dreaming up a widget that needs to be built and then inserting it into a business process. Data science problems are, by their nature, problems that require probing and investigation until the correct solution reveals itself.

The need to go through a process of investigating a problem necessitates that the initial stages of the project plan are somewhat open ended. You cannot plan deliverables until they are known. This ambiguity typically leaves project managers feeling very uncomfortable. Their discomfort will often manifest itself as a pressure toward defining a concrete deliverable, which by its nature means determining a solution before the problem is understood.

There are multiple other reasons why the important exploratory stages of a data science project will be neglected. The key message of this chapter is, do not let that happen. The more time you spend ensuring the problem is properly defined, the more likely your project will succeed. You will also spend less time scrambling to try and salvage a project that is off track. We start by focusing on the task of getting a clear statement of the problem.

Problem Statements

A common complaint made by data scientists is that it is difficult to get a client to give them a clear idea of the problem they want solved. We will shortly probe the reasons why the client might resist giving a clear definition. Before we do that, it is worthwhile emphasizing that **extracting a clear problem statement from a client is part of the data scientist's responsibility**. Much credence is given to the fact that data scientists have mathematical, programming, and business acumen. That business acumen should come to light in helping your client frame their problems in a way that can be solved with your technical skills. If there was one aspect of the entire process of doing data science that you could focus on to single-handedly improve the outcomes of data science projects, it is this: **get the problem well defined before doing anything else**.

This problem persists, in part, because it sounds so obvious it is assumed to be always true. Any project manager reading this could easily be thinking to themselves: *I focus much of my time on this because it is important, but, yes, I have seen other managers do that badly.* The "self-serving" cognitive bias for taking credit when we succeed and finding external causes when we fail is so well established, we should constantly be vigilant against it.[1] We tend to believe that our own work is well executed. So even if we recognize that a problem exists elsewhere, we are less likely to examine our own projects for such simple mistakes.

This is not unique to data science. Clear problem definitions are a common source of pain for many kinds of work. Complaints about this regularly come from engineers and graphic designers, in fact any discipline that involves trying to deliver something based on a client brief is prone to this issue. It is a complaint I continually hear from my friends and colleagues who are experienced software architects and developers. As software development has a great deal in common with data science,

---

[1] A.H. Mezulis, L.Y. Abramson, J.S. Hyde, and B.L. Hankin. 2004. "Is There a Universal Positivity Bias in Attributions? A Meta-Analytic Review of Individual, Developmental, and Cultural Differences in the Self-Serving Attributional Bias," *Psychological Bulletin* 130, pp. 711–747.

but is also a more mature field, it is worthwhile examining what is known about how to solve the problem in software development.

Reasons for Poor Definitions

In the world of software development, there is a rule of thumb that is often expressed as follows: *You should not start solution design until you have finished gathering requirements.* This expression is similar in spirit to the Charles Kettering quote used to open this chapter, but the emphasis is different. Mr. Kettering was expressing the underappreciated utility of taking the time to think clearly about the problem you want to solve. Software engineers are flatly refusing to entertain a solution until you tell them everything you need the software to do.

It is worth asking why this difference in emphasis exists. Some consider it a method of reducing downstream scope creep, meaning the gradual introduction of additional requirements that push out delivery and exceed budgets.[2] Which, in turn, can help reduce the potential for accrued technical debt.[3] But these are not the only reasons software engineers have needed to push back against a discussion on solutions until they are satisfied with the problem statement.

Software developers have expressed to me that this approach helps them manage upward against poor outcomes. They have described the experience of stakeholders pushing solution ideas onto a project, but then holding the developers responsible when the solution is inadequate. The rule of postponing solution discussion captures a push by the software engineering discipline to take responsibility for the outcomes of their projects. They do this by ensuring that the solution discussion is focused on the totality of requirements that define the problem, so that they can provide some guarantee of success.

---

[2] R. Larson, and E. Larson. 2009. "Top Five Causes of Scope Creep... and What to Do About Them," Project Management Institute Global Congress 2009.

[3] S. Watts, and J. Hertvik. July 30, 2020. "Technical Debt: The Ultimate Guide," *DevOps Blog BMC,* http://bmc.com/blogs/technical-debt-explained-the-complete-guide-to-understanding-and-dealing-with-technical-debt

If we take the software engineers at their word, we should then ask why it was that so often solutions were being offered before problems were completely defined. A complete answer to this question is likely to be complicated and nuanced, but there are several drivers that we can infer from principles of human behavior.

Consider first, that rigorously defining a problem is hard work. Forcing yourself to think about a business problem and documenting all its nuances is difficult. By comparison, imagining a piece of software that will solve the problem is far more enjoyable. This is a situation in which people appear to be following a path of least resistance. We are all continuously tempted to avoid difficult work by substituting it with another task that is less strenuous. Our tendency to avoid hard work is so strong that there is evidence our decisions themselves are influenced by the difficulty of acting on them.[4] Note, that this is not deliberate laziness, it involves subconscious biases and heuristics that we are usually unaware of. It is possible that problems are not being clearly defined because of an unconscious bias within management to avoid the difficult task of rigorous definition. Instead, that work is being substituted with the less demanding task of speculatively designing a solution.

In the world of data science, there are additional factors that will contribute to problems being underspecified, many of which are apparent from the way data science projects are mismanaged.[5] I will outline three of these reasons in detail: the mythology of data science, the opaque nature of our techniques, and the statistical literacy of management.

The first reason is a mythology suggesting data scientists are magicians who can take any data set and vague problem statement and weave an impressive technological solution. The hype surrounding the career, the shortage of people, and the panic to monetize data has meant that projects are started hastily with fuzzy expectations.

---

[4] N. Hagura, and P.H.J. Diedrichsen. February 2017. "Perceptual Decisions Are Biased by the Cost to Act," *eLife*. https://doi.10.7554/eLife.18422.001

[5] T. O'Toole. March 02, 2020. "What's the Best Approach to Data Analytics?" *Harvard Business Review*. https://hbr.org/2020/03/whats-the-best-approach-to-data-analytics

It is our responsibility as data scientists to take charge of this process, in much the same way that software engineers do. We need to build standards of engagement that will ensure that our skills are being suitably applied. The long-term effect of neglecting this problem can only be greater skepticism toward our discipline and either fewer job opportunities or greater constraints on our projects. Hence, it is in our best interests to ensure that poorly conceived projects are not allowed to continue.

The second reason that our projects are often underdefined is that, unlike software development, people generally have no preconceived idea of what the final output of a data science project will be. In other words, the practice of data science is opaque to outsiders. To those of us who work in the field it is easy to understand the general categories of outcomes, but we often struggle to explain them in a way that our clients seem to really understand. I routinely encounter people who conceive of all data science solutions as some form of clustering.

We know that the final outcomes can vary wildly. It might be a model that predicts the likelihood of a specific event and triggers an intervention. It may be a system that can automate decisions using live experimentation, online learning, or Thompson sampling.[6] Or it could be a graph-based inference algorithm for analyzing the root cause of failures in a manufacturing plant. These are all potential data science outputs, and they are all abstract things, involving part systems engineering, part statistics or machine learning, and part business case. In a very strong sense, you need to have a cursory understanding of the algorithms and methods in order to understand the output.

Most software, on the other hand, can be reasonably well characterized by the inputs and the outputs alone. These are exactly what the users see. Hence a user who possesses the patience to thoroughly outline what is required in terms of what will be entered and what will come out can describe most traditional software systems very well. The key difference is that they can do this without knowing anything about software or

---

[6] D. Russo, B. Van Roy, A. Kazerouni, I. Osband, and Z. Wen. 2018. "A Tutorial on Thompson Sampling," *Foundations and Trends in Machine Learning* 11, no. 1, pp. 1–96.

programming. This is not always true of traditional software, but it is almost never true of data science.

It is almost impossible to describe the outputs of a data science project without covering something about the algorithms. In a strong sense, when you describe the way inputs are turned into outputs **you are doing the data science**. More importantly, it is very difficult to even describe the required inputs and outputs without doing some of the data science. A significant portion of what we do as data scientists is understanding how to characterize the business problem as a set of inputs and outputs in order to get the desired result, including the trade-offs and biases in making certain kinds of decisions based on certain kinds of data. The net effect is when a stakeholder attempts to define the solution without understanding the algorithms, or having done the analysis, then it is likely to be misguided.

The third and final reason that data science projects are inadequately framed is that your business stakeholders and managers are not guaranteed to have a high level of statistical literacy. Despite the presence of statistics courses in most business degrees and MBA programs, management is not immune to the data literacy gap identified by Gartner.[7] Douglas Hubbard, the author of the book "How to measure anything," observes that previous academic exposure to statistics can nevertheless yield inadequate patterns of thought and interpretation of statistical techniques.[8]

The issue of insufficient statistical literacy among business stakeholders is not something we can correct overnight, and perhaps not ever. So, in order to deliver successful projects, we need to work around it. In other words, we need to have strategies that help us deliver the right outcomes, even though management may not understand some of the critical nuances of what we are doing. In a very pragmatic sense, our job is often about **helping people who don't really understand data to make better**

---

[7] K. Panetta. February 06, 2019. "A Data and Analytics Leader's Guide to Data Literacy," *Smarter with Gartner.* www.gartner.com/smarterwithgartner/a-data-and-analytics-leaders-guide-to-data-literacy

[8] D. Hubbard. 2014. *How to Measure Anything* (Third Edition, John Wiley & Sons, Inc.), p. 41.

decisions using data. I will return to talk about this specific problem in the coming chapters. For the moment, we shall focus on general strategies for solving the dilemma of poor problem definitions.

The issues discussed so far are all related to misunderstandings, inexperience, knowledge, and information gaps. A general solution to these problems is to nurture effective communication strategies, in particular communication with nontechnical people. Improving your ability to communicate with stakeholders is essential to getting good problem statements, and it will be the focus of the remainder of the chapter.

Managing Communication

In the preceding section, I gave several reasons why a project might be poorly outlined. It may be due to managerial pressure to undertake a data science project without a clear goal, or it could be because there is a genuine problem that is not well stated because the client has a limited understanding of either the problem itself or what possible solutions might look like. People will often limit the way they describe problems based on their expectations of what needs to be known in order to solve it. If those expectations are misguided, then way the problem is described might be misleading.

The key to resolving these issues is developing a strong communication channel with your client. This channel will help you understand their concerns and help them understand what you need to know. The better they understand what it is you will be doing, the more likely they will provide details that are relevant. They will also feel that they are participating in the process, which will raise trust levels. This will help you when there are difficult issues and decisions to discuss.

The fundamental goal is to help your clients understand what data science can realistically achieve. You almost always need to help them understand that data science is about solving very specific problems. You will need to explain that it may involve deliberately ignoring other problems in the process. You may need to explain the differences between techniques and the trade-offs between them. In the process of doing this, they can see how the specifics of the problem statement impact the way it is solved and the effectiveness of the solution.

Communication skills are critical across the entire project life cycle, but probably most critical at these early stages. For our current purposes we are aiming to get our client or stakeholder to understand that the more time they take to ensure that the problem is well defined, and expectations made explicit, the more likely they will get a successful outcome. That sounds all well and good, you might ask, but how do we do that?

I am going to discuss three very general rhetorical tools you can use: stories, analogies, and concrete examples. They may not always be appropriate, but hopefully as we discuss why they work you will see ways to adapt and adjust them to your situation.

Telling Stories

It is no exaggeration to say that stories are one of the fundamental ways that human beings consume information. There is something inherent in narrative structures that help us understand and remember ideas. Competitive memorizers will describe the methods by which they commit large amounts of information to memory through the construction of a memory palace, which contains a form of narrative.[9] Story telling has been investigated as a pedagogical tool for enhancing recall,[10] and has been shown to improve the accuracy and longevity of what we learn and may be due to the listener engagement that the story commands.[11]

Remembering that we are looking for communication strategies that will help improve the definition of the data science problem, we can ask: how will stories help us?

We have several options. If you already have specific experiences with a type of problem or industry that is related to your current engagement, then you could use these experiences. The previous projects can be woven

[9] B. Handwerk. March 13, 2017. "Neuroscientists Unlock the Secrets of Memory Champions," *Smithsonian Magazine*. https://smithsonianmag.com

[10] T. Oaks. 1995. "Storytelling: A Natural Mnemonic: A Study of a Storytelling Method to Positively Influence Student Recall of Instruction," [PhD Dissertation]. University of Tennessee. https://trace.tennessee.edu/utk_graddiss/2540

[11] V. Borris. December 20, 2017. "What Makes Storytelling So Effective For Learning?" *Harvard Business Review*. www.harvardbusiness.org/what-makes-story telling-so-effective-for-learning/

into a story where you highlight the critical details that needed to be known in the discovery phase in order to get the right outcome. Of course, you cannot betray the confidence of former clients, but, if possible, you can talk directly about why certain details that they omitted had a significant impact on a project result. This is a delicate balance, not in the least of which because it potentially involves admitting you worked on a project with some degree of failure or setback.

If you do not have this direct experience, or nothing that you can reveal, then it is worthwhile scanning literature for case studies and examples where these details are revealed. There are often books that focus on the application of various data science techniques to a particular domain. They will contain more detailed case studies than general data science books. For example, the book *Artificial Intelligence for Security* provides a concise introduction to the terminology and problems faced in organizational security, and a set of machine learning approaches to solving these problems.[12] The book *Highly Effective Marketing Analytics* presents an overview of the primary terminology in data-driven marketing and a discussion of data science approaches that can be used.[13]

An alternative strategy is to use the vehicle of a story to reflect to your client the understanding you have gleaned from your requirements gathering. For example, the way you reflect via a story could be like this:

Let me just repeat back to you my understanding so far. When a potential new customer comes to your website, they need to fill in an application form that consists of 3 different screens. On the final screen they will submit a document for review. They then receive a confirmation e-mail and an application ID. The application will be added to a queue that will then raise it to the manual review team...

---

[12] A. Addo, S. Centhala, and M. Shanmugam. 2020. *Artificial Intelligence for Security* (New York, NY: Business Expert Press).
[13] M. Hu. 2020. *Highly Effective Marketing Analytics* (New York, NY: Business Expert Press).

This is very dry as far as stories go and not very entertaining. However, by taking what you have learned from a client and reflecting it back to them as a narrative that respects the order in which things take place you will force them to think about it this way. One thing that it can help with is ensuring that missing details emerge. When the client hears a description of the process with key details missing, they will feel compelled to add them to the story. They will also notice if some parts do not make sense. If there is a missing logical connection between events in the story, they will often either add them immediately, if known, or volunteer to find them out.

The process I have described in the previous paragraph will help you use people's desire for narrative to get them to volunteer details. One key difficulty of employing this process is getting the opportunity to use it. By which I mean finding the right point in the dialogue to engage the client with a narrative reflecting what you have learned.

Very often technical people find themselves in a conversation that is dominated by the business stakeholders. The conversation will take a variety of twists and turns until it has covered everything the stakeholders want to discuss. **You need to cultivate a sense of comfort with interrupting them**. Apologize as profusely as needed and take the time to explain that you want to make sure you have understood. Then use this opportunity to reflect everything that they have said using the narrative structure ideas presented earlier. Careful interruption and then reflection by paraphrasing in a narrative structure is a very successful strategy for collecting complete information and identifying hidden details and assumptions.

Using Analogy

Previously we discussed the idea of using stories to present ideas and ensure that the logic and sequence of events was consistent and complete. Unfortunately, not all ideas can be easily expressed through narratives. Sometimes your role as a data scientist will require you to communicate about some highly sophisticated concepts.

One of the most powerful tools you have to help people understand something new very quickly is an analogy. There is a reason why these are universal tools in textbooks and classrooms around the world. Our minds seem more able to process new concepts as variations of something familiar than as purely abstract descriptions. Analogy is a tool that allows us to develop intuitions about domains that we have no direct experience of. Although analogies can be stretched too far, resulting in misunderstandings, so they need to be carefully chosen to aid comprehension.[14]

It is very likely that everyone reading this book would have initially learned key ideas about electricity (such as voltage, current, and resistance) using the analogy of water. Your teacher took something you understood well (small children love to play with buckets of water and pipes, at least mine do) and then used your intuitions about it to teach you about something you cannot see: the behavior of electrons.

A simple and effective tool for improving your communication with nontechnical people is to maintain a library of analogies. For example, I have often been faced with the task of explaining why, when choosing which model to use, we can't have a model that is best in all testing scenarios. Clients might struggle to understand that there is an element of randomness that is always present. An analogy that works here is sports teams. Ask your client who they think is the best team in their favorite sport. Ask them why. Do they win more games than any other team? Then ask them if that team always wins, to which the answer will inevitably be "no." You can then explain that statistical models are the same, the best model is the one that wins more often than others, but it is not guaranteed to be the best in all situations. Moreover, just like in sport, it is very difficult to predict which model will perform best on any given day. Generally, we look at who will win most over the long term.

You can also use analogy when clients ask about the details of a particular technique. For example, if you needed to explain how k-means clustering works you could use magnets and ball bearings as an analogy. The data set is like a table covered with ball bearings and the algorithm is like a process that places magnets at key locations. The ball bearings will move across the table, being influenced by the positions of the magnets

---

[14] M.K. Orgill, and G. Bodner. 2004. "What Research Tells Us About Using Analogies to Teach Chemistry," *Chemistry Education: Research and Practice* 5, no. 1, pp. 12–32.

as well as the other ball bearings. The ball bearings form small groups that grow as more ball bearings are attracted to them. In the end, we have several clusters across the table equal to the number of magnets. We can look at the relative sizes of the groups and draw conclusions about that part of the table.

Unfortunately, analogies are not always easily constructed for a specific technique. Generally, they will leave out some key properties (as the aforementioned clustering analogy does) in order to be rendered into the analogical domain. Which means that they can be misleading for the simple reason that not all aspects of two systems will be analogous. What they do achieve is to give an initial understanding of what a process or technique is doing by exploiting certain intuitions and shared understanding. You should take the time to develop good analogies for some of the key technologies you use regularly. Revise them if you see common misunderstandings or develop a narrative to address specific aspects of the analogy that are not genuinely analogous.

Concrete Examples

Often the only way to understand something difficult is through experiencing it ourselves. In the absence of direct experience, it can be helpful if someone takes the time to outline a concrete and specific example. Note, that the type of concrete example matters. There may be a mathematical derivation or proof for some difficult idea you want to convey. But that is unlikely to be an effective tool for helping a nontechnical audience understand. The type of example I mean is a worked use case from the business domain.

Concrete examples help with concepts that may not be intuitively accessible or when the key insight involves a shift in thinking about a key issue. Take, for example, the issue of helping a client to understand the importance of choosing the right metric to measure the success of a solution. How do you get someone to understand that if a prediction problem is highly unbalanced, that overall predictive accuracy is a misleading and uninformative metric?

The issue could be that your client uses the term accuracy without knowing that it has a specific technical definition. The existence of words that have an everyday usage and a technical definition can create frustrating communication problems. Your first task when faced with this situation should be to ensure that your client understands how accuracy is calculated. Once you have this shared understanding of what accuracy means, you may find that the client still doesn't understand why it is not always a useful way to measure performance. This will likely be because they have never had to consider what imbalance in the data means.

Giving a specific example is the only way I know to demonstrate the complexity of this issue to nonmathematical people. In large part, because the conclusion is somewhat counterintuitive, our natural inclination is to think something like the following: surely accuracy is simple, something is either more or less accurate.

I have had this exact sentiment expressed to me multiple times by multiple different managers. When faced with this situation you need to illustrate that their intuitions are wrong, and direct examples are fantastic for this job. Here is how you might use a concrete example to dispel this misunderstanding:

Imagine that you need to identify which of your customers is going to cancel their subscription in the next month. You have one million customers, and you know that roughly one thousand of them will cancel. Those thousand customers represent 0.1 percent of your customer base.

Now if you have a model that, when asked if a customer is going to cancel, always responds "NO," then it will have an accuracy of 99.9%. However, if you had a model that identified 500 of those who would cancel, and mistakenly identified 2,000 of those who would not cancel then its predictive accuracy would be 99.8%.

The first model has the highest accuracy, but it is clearly not useful at all, while the second model has some potential. This demonstrates clearly why accuracy is the wrong metric to compare solutions for this problem.

The concrete example above allows you to go right to the heart of the matter and illustrate to your client why their intuitions might be wrong.

It also provides you an ideal opportunity to introduce alternative metrics such as sensitivity or specificity. The concrete example is far more persuasive than relying on your authority, or by referring to theory or standard practice. Examples give the client something that their own minds can chew over and come to terms with.

Of course, not every issue that will arise in a project can be communicated through stories, analogies, or examples. Some aspects of the job are inherently complicated. Getting a client to understand the bias/variance dilemma is one that I have personally struggled with. The more difficult and complicated the project, the more likely there will be subtleties that are difficult to convey and discuss.

In the end you will need to build trust with your client so that you do not need to explain every mundane detail. One of the best ways you can do that is to focus on explaining the things that you can explain well. By bringing the stakeholder into our world, you will make them feel involved, and more inclined to trust you on some of the more difficult to explain issues.

I am not suggesting that communication is straightforward, in fact contrary to many people's opinions, I believe it is the hardest part of this kind of work. The best I can recommend is that you spend some time becoming comfortable with using tactful interruption and paraphrasing, then develop a set of analogies and examples that correspond to the kinds of techniques you tend to use and refine them. Ensuring that you understand your client and they understand the main issues will significantly increase the likelihood that your project is a success.

Getting Clearer Problem Statements

In the preceding discussion, about the role of communication in managing your client, I did not answer the core question of how to get the clear problem statement. A clear communication strategy is a requirement and an ingredient, rather than a complete solution. To get to a clear problem definition normally requires multiple iterations in which you increasingly help your client understand why the current statement of the problem is not specific enough. In each iteration, you will focus on one part of the definition, illustrating what is unclear about it and working with your client to improve it.

To take my own advice I will give you a crude, but hopefully illustrative, example. Your client has initially come to you and said: "We need to solve customer churn."

If your instinct is to laugh out loud, I can assure you that I, and colleagues of mine, have received client briefs that are no more sophisticated than this. There are many ways in which such a problem definition could be improved. At this point we do not know how big the problem is, if there are existing systems to prevent it. We do not know what the potential methods are that could be employed to prevent churn and their associated costs. We do not know what solving it might mean (both practically and in terms of how it might be measured). In short, although we know vaguely the general domain of the problem, we have no way to determine if a potential solution will be an improvement over the status quo. So, how might we take the client from that vague statement to a definition for which we could unambiguously evaluate a result?

The received wisdom in data science tutorials is that you always start by looking at the data. This is how many people I know would start a problem with such a vague definition. They would ask for the data associated with the churn and examine it for themselves.

This is particularly useful if the client has revealed that, aside from the existence of the problem, they know nothing about it. Even if the client makes certain claims about the nature of the problem, it is essential that you confirm those claims for yourself. You do not want to get caught up solving a problem that does not exist.

However, there are reasons to consider prolonging the problem definition stage before asking to see any data. For example, you may discover that there were multiple previous efforts to solve the problem, by building models to predict churn and then sending e-mails to those customers with a discount or something similar. In which case, it is likely that the problem is not about identifying potential churners (presuming previous models were not completely random) but about improving the intervention, which may require an altogether different approach. If you blindly started building the next churn model in the series, unaware that the problem is with the effectiveness of the intervention and not with identifying those who will churn, then your project is no more likely to succeed than the previous projects.

You may think that the fault in the previous example lies on the shoulders of the managers or stakeholders who engaged our hypothetical data scientist. To some extent that is true, however, I would like you to take a broader view of what data science is. It is not just building models and algorithms, it is about understanding the fundamental nature of problems, so that the models and algorithms you build can be used to interact with the world to solve those problems. The client in the previous example may not be aware that there is a separation between being able to predict something and being able to influence it. It is our job to identify these situations and help our clients understand why their projects have been failing.

The advantage of knowing how the data is being generated and the existing processes that operate in the problem space is enormous. Which is why I would recommend that the first line of questioning when faced with an ambiguous problem statement is to discover exactly these things, rewind from the problem statement, and unpack how the data surrounding the problem emerges. These questions are relatively simple, so to extend our churn example we might ask the following series of questions:

"What are you currently doing to prevent churn?"
"Have you done anything different in the past?"
"How do you measure and quantify the problem?"
"How is that data collected?"

You need only replace with word churn with whatever your client's problem is, and you will have an introductory question sequence. As your client answers these questions you may find that it leads naturally to new questions. For example, the client could respond to the first question as follows: "We send an e-mail to all customers who have not visited the site in 2 months with an offer of 10% off their next purchase." We could ask the following series of follow-up questions:

"What percentage of those customers take up the offer?"

"How was 2 months chosen as the period? Have you tried other periods?"

"How was 10% chosen as the offer amount? Have you tried other incentives?"

"What percentage of those customers churn?"

These questions lead you naturally deeper into the problem domain. They should continue until such time as you feel comfortable that you understand the exact circumstances of the problem.

In this instance, the example I have used of a vague problem statement comes from a class of problems that all data scientists should be familiar with, the problem of customer churn. Even though it takes many forms, customer churn is a ubiquitous business problem that you are likely to be familiar with. Prior exposure to the class of problem will make the process of generating questions and refining the project easier. That will not always be the case, you should expect to encounter problems where you do not have a readily prepared set of questions to ask. Here are some guidelines for a general questioning process.

Precise Problem Statement

The goal of initial questioning is to get the most general statement of the problem. For example: "What is the business problem you are trying to solve?" You may get very vague and uninformative responses to this question, so then probe deeper with questions like: "What is the exact circumstance in which the problem occurs?" This could be about the business units involved, subsets of customers, specific teams, regions, or the underlying systems.

In general, you should try and narrow the problem down across any or all of the following dimensions: people, places, time, processes, products (services), and systems. But do not be limited by these options, asking any questions that attempt to narrow a problem tend to help surface critical details.

Expected Path of Change

If the problem statement remains unclear or seems too wide in scope, it can be easier to ask how the client expects things to change. For example, you might ask: "What aspect of the business will be changed when the problem is solved?" or "How will you know if the problem is solved?" This should clearly demarcate which behaviors or outcomes are deemed problematic.

This approach is still about attempting to narrow the scope, it is just an alternative strategy. If the client cannot immediately define the boundaries and limitations of the problem, they may be able to define them for what they are expecting in a solution. Note, that we are not asking them to define the solution explicitly, but just boundaries or limitations to that solution.

Avoid Solutions

The danger in the previous approach is that it can put the client in a solutions mindset. You need to be wary of problem statements that are in reality descriptions of solutions. For example, "We need to build a recommendation system to improve customer retention." This statement conflates a problem with a solution. Your task here is to try and get the client to recognize that the problem is customer retention, and they are proposing the solution: a recommendation system.

The distinction between placing boundaries on a solution versus receiving a solution statement resides in the degree of prescription. Here is an example: "We need to solve customer retention, but it has to be done through marketing and service channels. The backlog for the product team is too long to solve it through product changes." This statement places expectations on the solution, driven by the practical reality of the business context. But unlike the previous request to build a recommendation system, it does not define an explicit solution.

Separate Conflated Problems

Be on the lookout for multiple conflated problems. Your client may say something like: "We need to identify more high quality and loyal customers to grow our business and improve the profitability."

This type of business jargon problem statement is very common. It contains multiple conflated problems and objectives. You should try and get the client to recognize that there are two problems here, they want to identify leads to grow the business, and they want to identify leads that will improve profitability. It may turn out that the lead generation component can be separated out and used to solve the first problem. Profitability may be solved in the same solution, or it may require something different. Separation of the distinct problems will allow you to bring the most appropriate solution to each problem. In this example, the problem statement also contains an embedded solution, that is, that the path to profitability improvement is via lead generation.

Iterate

Getting clear problem statements is not a linear process. You will likely find yourself iteratively applying these approaches in response to your client's answers. If you are patient and follow it through you should have one or more very clear and distinct problem statements. They should be separate from requested solutions and easy to identify how and where they affect the business. With all of that in place, you can comfortably look at the data and be somewhat certain you are looking at the right data to try and solve the right problem. These themes we have discussed so far will continue to recur throughout the discussion.

Getting to this point does not mean that the problem is yet perfectly defined, there are nuances to any problem that will affect what kind of solution you might deliver. These issues tend to fall into three categories: the kinds of actions that can be taken, the timing of those actions, and the relative costs/rewards of all action outcome scenarios. I will deal with these issues in the following chapters. After which I will return to discuss an alternative reason why you might find that the client is avoiding defining the problem and is instead driving for a predetermined solution.

Summary

Data science as a discipline is about solving difficult problems and achieving outcomes for your clients. A large part of your role is to help nontechnical or nonstatistically minded people understand why not all ways of presenting statistics and building models are valid. Building a common understanding between yourself and the client about the right way to approach the problem needs to be part of your process from the very first meeting.

Typically, it will take time to get good at communication, but there are three things you can focus on to improve. Practice paraphrasing what you have heard. Develop analogies to explain techniques you use. Prepare concrete examples that illustrate problems or pitfalls in the projects you work on. If you can do all of this and make it second nature, you will find it easier to get clearer problem definitions.

Key Points:

1. Clear problem definitions are critical to successful data science projects.
2. There are many reasons why problems are not well defined, but often a knowledge gap and poor communication are involved.
3. Developing a library of analogies and examples that help you communicate will go a long way to getting shared understanding and trust.
4. Stories allow you illustrate key points and reflect what you have been told in a sequential narrative that encourages clients to fill in details.
5. Take your client through a process of systematic questions to clarify the context of the problem.
6. Learn to be comfortable politely interrupting to clarify points and paraphrase what has been said.
7. Looking at the data before you have clarity on the problem you are solving may be a waste of time.

CHAPTER 2

Project Parameters

When you are taking the client through the process of framing the problem, there are multiple general scenarios that regularly occur despite all the superficial differences between companies and industries. These scenarios tend to be driven by a small number of fundamental parameters that define and constrain the project. You should be able to use these parameters to guide your thinking about the approach to take. In this chapter, we will discuss three of these key parameters: predecessors to the project, hard thresholds in the decision context, and the degree to which the project is problem or data driven.

Predecessor Projects

The first critical aspect that determines the type of project is whether the work has a predecessor. This may be an existing business process that generates the desired outcome (albeit with less than desirable efficiency or effectiveness), prior analytical work, or production models that you are expected to extend. It should be thoroughly clear to you whether the project has a pure business precedent, an analytical precedent, or there is no prior analysis or process upon which it needs to depend or build.

If you are told a project has no predecessor, be sure to question this thoroughly. There can sometimes be hidden predecessor projects or processes that are not discussed because they are deemed unworthy, or an outright embarrassment. They may be excluded from the discussion because of subpar performance, or because of failed attempts at deployment. It is also possible that the predecessors are being obscured to make a difficult project seem more palatable.

The value in uncovering predecessors is multifaceted. The notes and results of such projects can be a gold mine of information, or they could be a critical red flag that the project is untenable. The existence of a hidden predecessor will mean that there are unspoken benchmarks that your work will be measured against.

In many cases, the predecessor project will be the business process that generates the data you will be using. In this case the baseline is transparent, it is the performance of the status quo. A more difficult situation is when your work will result in such a significant change in the business process that the performance will not be directly comparable with the past. In that case, we need to rely on a thorough understanding of the business process thresholds, discussed next.

Hard Thresholds

The second critical aspect that will define the scope of your initial work is the existence of hard thresholds. For example, does a system need to achieve a predetermined level of accuracy in order to be economically viable. A simple (and unrealistic) example of which would be predicting movements in a stock market, you need the predicted movements to be large enough that when combined with the calibrated probabilities, the expected return is larger than the transaction costs. Knowing these hard thresholds will help you identify quickly how close each iteration is to economic feasibility.

Another example of hard thresholds would be the acceptable error rate in fraud prediction. If you are providing a system to detect fraud, you need the business to understand that the system will make mistakes, and they need to articulate the acceptable thresholds. It may take time to get them to understand that there is a trade-off between missing some fraud (false negatives) and mistakenly irritating genuine customers (false positives). The business will always have a limit to their appetite for the later. The stakeholders may focus discussion on ensuring that all of the fraud is identified and avoiding all false negatives, but you also need to determine their tolerance for false positives.

Hard thresholds may not be known explicitly by the business. By which I mean if you ask directly they will not have an answer, but if you present them with a scenario, they will be able to tell you whether it is viable. You may need to play a cat and mouse game of posing scenarios and having them shot down in order to find where these hard thresholds are.

Data Versus Business Problems

The final critical parameter that constrains your focus is where the project lies on the data versus business problem dimension. All data science projects lie somewhere on the scale of being either entirely problem driven (here is the problem we need you to solve, use whatever data you can), to entirely data driven (here is some data, try and find a way to leverage it). In general, they are rarely at the extremes.

Luckily, the general direction of this parameter should be obvious by the way the client talks about the project. Are they emphasizing a particular problem or a particular data set? You need to be careful and ask sufficient questions to ensure you understand how success of the project will be measured. I have seen many times a client that dominates the discussion with talk of a particular data set, only to turn around and judge the project by whether a particular business problem has been solved. We will talk more about this later, but clients often become single minded about utilizing a particular data resource (possibly because it was part of the business-case they used to raise funds for the project), even though it is not the most important aspect of the project.

If you are told the project can use any available data, then you need to get an idea of what is available. First at a high level of just knowing what the data sets are and how (or if) they are connected. You will dig into the details of each one later, but at first you need to grasp the scale of the resources you will have available, and how well they connect to the problem you are trying to solve.

If you are presented with a pure data problem, that is, one in which the business cares only about finding applications for a given data set, then the way you think about the business problem becomes very different. You still need to pose a solution to a problem, but it may be one that the business is not currently thinking about, or it may be a customer problem that allows you to define a new data-driven product line or feature.

I have given these pure data projects less emphasis in this book because they are rare. In addition, it is harder to give general advice. In some sense, you will need to take on the role of a business owner yourself and ask questions about how the business functions to identify problems and opportunities yourself. For the remainder of the book, we will presume that there is some specific business problem to which your project is aligned.

Summary

We have discussed three critical parameters that influence the nature and direction of the project: what are the predecessors or existing processes, what are the hard thresholds, and is the project dominated by a problem or a data set. The first two of these three parameters tells you the benchmarks you will be measured against. If you are lucky enough to have them both clearly defined, then you have a clear view of the gap you need to cover, from the precedent of the existing system to the hard threshold of where it needs to be. If the existing system is already meeting the threshold, then the threshold acts as an optimization boundary. It tells you the lines you cannot cross when pursuing a solution to the essential problem. A comprehensive understanding of these two aspects of the project also tells you how realistic the budget and timeline is.

The final parameter gives you an indication of the resources you are expected to use. The client may have indicated you are free to bring in new data sets as needed, but this is generally time consuming. You want to understand the data resource limitations you will face when you start, and you want to know how well they represent the problem space. This will also indicate how realistic the client is.

If you are having difficulty getting any of these three aspects of the project clarified, and you are making every effort to communicate clearly and patiently, then it is possible there is resistance to your project. This resistance can take many forms and is discussed in the next chapter about getting buy-in from your stakeholders.

CHAPTER 3

Getting Buy-In

Sometimes we find ourselves facing a client who insists that the proper problem statement is in fact a definition of a solution. In other words, there was some process that preceded your arrival, which determined what the problem was and what the solution should be. It is usually not immediately apparent whether the proposed solution is appropriate, or if it will even work. This situation is symptomatic of a client or organization that is not bought into data science as a problem-solving process.

This chapter is about identifying why clients will resist including you in all stages and getting the buy-in you will need to identify the right problem, the right solution, and all the relationships you need to implement it. The process of getting buy-in usually begins with getting various people to share enough information with you to thoroughly evaluate the nature of the problem.

Management studies have long identified that critical information about the feasibility of projects can be held back from stakeholders. There are a range of reasons that the so-called employee voice can be withheld, including organizational culture, leadership styles, and employee personality.[1] Recent studies have investigated the effect of information sharing and availability among front-line staff as an impediment to voice.[2] Perhaps more importantly, it has been discovered that the extent of known

---

[1] Y. Yang. 2020. "Understanding the Antecedents of Employee Voice: A Review of the Literature," *Japan Journal of Human Resource Management* 21, no. 2, pp. 58–86.

[2] I. Hussain, R. Shu, S. Tangirala, and S. Ekkirala. 2019. "The Voice Bystander Effect: How Information Redundancy Inhibits Employee Voice," *Academy of Management Journal* 62, no. 3, pp. 828–849. https://doi.org/10.5465/amj.2017.0245

data points about a flawed project influence the likelihood of those problems being voiced.[3]

As a data scientist, you will be faced with attempting to extract information about business problems from people with varying degrees of willingness to share. You may be an outside consultant, or a data scientist from an internal team, either way you are likely to be viewed as an outsider. In addition, you will be faced with your own decisions about when to voice concerns to your stakeholders. The complexity of the problem and the variety and availability of key information is going to influence your ability to evaluate the situation and your options for moving forward.

This chapter is predicated on the idea that you believe, as I do, that the proper role of data science is understanding the real business problem sufficiently that you can deliver the right solution. This may be exactly what the client is asking for, or it may be something different. To achieve this, it is critical that you are involved in the framing of the problem. If the project is ill-conceived, then you will be able to articulate the issues and provide alternatives.

To do this well, you need multiple people to buy into the idea of an end-to-end data science process. You need them to include you in the entire project scoping process. Unfortunately, this often means working your way backward to understand the extent to which decisions have already been made.

As this chapter is focused on dealing with different parts of an organization, I will use some specific terminology for issues faced with different teams. The term *client* is used to refer to the entire organization or business division you are working for. In other words, when the point being made is not about a specific part of the organization. The term *sponsors* will be used for the decision makers who have engaged you for the project (typically a senior level of management), while the term *operational staff* will be used to refer to front-line workers, team managers, or operational staff who are responsible for the line of business your project engages with.

---

[3] D.A. Shepherd, H. Patzelt, and C.M. Berry. 2019. "Why Didn't You Tell Me? Voicing Concerns Over Objective Information About a Project's Flaws," *Journal of Management* 45, no. 3, pp. 1087–1113.

Hidden Expectations

In the preceding chapters, we have discussed the dangers of premature solution design and some potential motivations and drivers for this situation. We attempted to solve some of this through communication strategies that will help the client understand why the problem may need further clarification. One of the key distinctions you will need to make early on is the extent to which the client has fixed ideas about what the solution might look like. This is straightforward when they have been explicit about it from the start. Other times, you might find that these expectations are hidden and not revealed until you begin to work on the project. In order to avoid uncovering the expectations too late in the process, it is worthwhile posing some hypotheticals early on. The goal of which is not to suggest solutions directly, but to probe around the edges of what a solution might look like. For example:

> "Would we be able to include a one-off survey in the customer log-in process?"
> "Are we able to change the structure of the sign-up form?"
> "Can we modify the pricing structure as part of a solution?"

You do not want your client to get locked on to thinking about a particular outcome. As we have discussed previously, this is often a source of problems. However, there is an advantage to discussing potential properties of a solution at a broad and general level, as it can help surface hidden expectations about the outcomes. These expectations may be hidden because the client has not thought about certain specifics, or because they consider them too obvious to mention.

To mitigate the danger of an early high-level solution discussion, you can present multiple hypothetical suggestions. Be sure to make each of them very general. Your goal is not to solve the problem or set the client on a particular train of thought, but to uncover any hidden expectations about what a solution might look like. If this strategy fails to reveal any expectations, then you can be reasonably certain that they do not exist.

If this potential solution discussion reveals expectations, then you need to identify the driving force behind those expectations. Often this is due to hard constraints that exist beyond the problem. For example, your client may be part of a company division that does not have the power or mandate to make structural changes to the company website or key systems. Alternatively, the restriction may be due to costs, your client may say that changing the operational processes for their support staff is off limits because the cost is too high (changing training manuals, support software, and going through retraining). These are both very useful things to discover because they may influence your thinking when you are exploring the data and running experiments or building models.

Alternatively, you may discover that the client has a fixed expectation about the solution because they have done their own research, or hired a previous consultant, or they have read a report about a particular technology. These situations are very tricky, you will need to simultaneously evaluate how well the client understands the solution they are suggesting, the nature of the problem they are trying to solve, and the extent to which the suggested solution could solve the problem.

Once you understand what the client's expectations are, either implicit or explicit, you can begin assessing them and attempting to influence them if needed. Achieving influence in an organization is a difficult process; in this book, we recommend a general strategy of building trust through clear communication and discussion. However, you should be aware that there will always be situations in which you will find it difficult to sway a key decision. In these situations, we need a variety of strategies for moving forward.

Knowledge and Responsibility

When faced with a dubious or uncertain looking project, you could choose just to go ahead and implement the requested solution. The danger is that a large portion of the responsibility for any failure will be assigned to you. It may not be explicit blame, but you should not underestimate the power of reputation in this industry. For the sake of self-interest, you should be communicating any concerns you have. On the other hand, you should not make pessimism your standard mind set. I have known some highly skeptical data scientists who have gained a negative reputation for saying every idea is going to fail.

To give good advice you will need to evaluate and calibrate your perspective. Sometimes risks need to be taken in business. Project sponsors are generally open to discussing the risks in a project, and your input can help them manage the risk reward trade-off. One way to encourage productive conversation is to explain the risks you have identified and label them with some metric of severity.

It is critical to remember that your long-term focus should be on building trust and credibility with your stakeholders. The worst approach is telling them that their ideas will not work, and then saying the equivalent of "I told you so," when things go wrong. A much better strategy is to identify the risks, then present either alternatives or fallback plans. The latter of which gives you a way to try what the client is asking for, but still deliver some value when and if it fails.

Many data scientists, and indeed technical people of different persuasions, will react very negatively to situations where they are pushed to implement something that they feel will not work. There is something deeply frustrating to technical people to be unable to persuade others of something that seems obvious to them. The mindset of clinging to frustration with your client should be avoided at all costs. It can create adversarial relationships between teams, or with managers and sponsors. In its place you should cultivate empathy for their perspectives. Focus on remembering that the work we do is difficult. It has likely taken you many years to become comfortable with the techniques in your repertoire. Remember this investment you have made and honor it by treating those without your understanding with empathy.

Of course, empathy is not enough to solve these problems, but it does give a foundation for constructive communication. Ultimately, to succeed in these scenarios we need strategies for dealing with the problems caused by different levels of understanding and various perspectives of what is achievable. You can be upfront about what you think without being dismissive. As discussed before, provide your client with well-reasoned arguments for the risks involved, and as many alternatives as possible.

One of the more difficult challenges you might face is that early on in a project you may not know enough to suggest a viable alternative. There may be a simple and fundamental reason why a proposed project is likely to fail, but without sufficient context it can be impossible to identify an alternative. In this situation, you should strive to explain the nature of the problem clearly, perhaps drawing on previous experience or case studies. In place of an alternative, you can outline the information you need to collect in order to develop alternatives. This strategy makes it clear to the project sponsors that you are looking for alternatives and being clear with them about what is needed.

Another general solution to the problem of being presented with a poorly conceived project is to engage the sponsors in a dialogue that helps them come to the same realization. In many instances, this can happen by showing them that there is a causal disconnect between what they are proposing and the outcome they are expecting.

Causal Disconnect

A very common reason that premature solutions fail is a causal disconnect between the data science work and the expected results. Here is a simple example to illustrate what we mean by a causal disconnect. Suppose you have been asked to improve customer satisfaction with your organization's phone support system by building a model to SMS-recommended articles in the company's FAQ, based on the description or keywords given over the phone support line. You build the system as requested and user testing indicates that the recommendations are closely aligned with user queries. However, when the model goes to production you discover that no one clicks on those recommendations, because most users select to speak to an operator shortly after arriving on the phone menu.

In this scenario, you have followed the suggested solution to a problem, which on the surface appears reasonable. In doing so, you have built a system that does what was asked but does not solve the problem. This example is simple for the sake of illustration, but it demonstrates a very common outcome for situations in which the client brings you a conceptual solution to a problem and you do not engage them in a dialogue about the context surrounding that core problem.

It may not be obvious from the project description whether the requested solution will work. So, we need to ask *why do projects like this fail?* A large part of the answer involves the depth of the causal reasoning that has gone into the solution. In the example given, the client suggests a solution in which the causal chain appears to be the following:

- Customer Unhappy
- Customer Calls Support Line
- Customer Describes Problem
- System sends Article by SMS
- Customer Reads Article
- Customer Satisfied

We are fooled into thinking this will work, because we understand how the proposed action could solve the customer problem. In fact, in some situations this solution might work. What we haven't done is ask whether the chain of causal events is such that this action can be effective. A discussion of the problem context allows us to build a deeper causal chain. In this example, we might develop something like the following:

- Customer Calls Support Line
  [~2K/Mnth]
- Customer Presented Options:
  [Product Help | Account | Installation | Operator]
- Customer makes a choice:
  [2 percent | 2 percent | 3 percent | 93 percent]
- If choice = Product Help then:
  Customer Describes Problem
  System sends Article by SMS
  Customer Reads Article
  Customer Satisfied [< 2 percent]

Building the chain of events through context gathering now illustrates for us that the proposed solution cannot make a large impact on the problem. Note, that the critical insight comes not just from understanding the sequence of events, but from understanding the alternative pathways, and the quantification of how many customers move through each path of the branching structure. This information may not be readily available in your initial meeting, but it is something you should push for. Quantification of what happens at each stage of a process will often reveal subtle difficulties in a proposed solution.

The process of building a comprehensive analysis of this kind is hard work and, although this example has been almost trivial, there are many ways that real-world scenarios can contain subtle problems that prevent solutions being effective. The process of gathering sufficient contextual information to evaluate a solution requires attention and practice. However, the first step is almost always the same, you need to get the client to rewind, and start at the beginning.

Rewind From Solutions

In situations where the client is prescribing a solution, the first step toward a clear problem statement is getting the client to rewind. Clients are likely to have jumped forward to a solution for a range of reasons, but that usually includes some combination of genuine interest in data science and a feeling that they need to be contributing to the solution because, after all, that is part of their job. This latter reason may be merely a feeling of responsibility, or it may be driven by fear. Fear that if they let some outside data scientist re-engineer their business processes, they may start to look unnecessary.

There are many different emotional reactions that drive the behavior of people inside organizations.[4] The fear that an employee's career is threatened has been identified as a common source of resistance to change, that is best mitigated by participation in the process.[5] Data science and analytics projects are just as susceptible to these fear-based social mechanisms that impede projects. We need to be careful to not assume that these attitudes are irrational, organizations are entirely capable of designing data-driven processes that measure the wrong things and hold

---

[4] R.M. Kanter. September 25, 2012. *Ten Reasons People Resist Change*, Harvard Business Review.
[5] L. Quast. November 26, 2012. "Overcome The 5 Main Reasons People Resist Change," Forbes Magazine.

employees accountable for outcomes beyond their control.[6] Instead, we should understand the sources of fear and seek to mitigate them.

To understand why fear emerges in your clients, you need to step back and think about what it is that we do. In the most abstract sense, data science is about optimizing processes by leveraging data. This sounds straightforward and innocuous. However, those processes we are optimizing are made up of the jobs of one or more people. When we are hired, typically by a higher-level manager, we are being implicitly told that the computational and statistical techniques we use should be able to discover better ways of doing these jobs than the people who currently do them.

You and I know that it is not so simple. Although the techniques we use are sometimes cutting edge, they are not capable of solving all problems. We know that applying them is very task specific and depends heavily on the domain knowledge of the people in the existing business process. However, the people doing these jobs do not know any of these things. From their perspective, an outsider with a laptop has been hired to come in and write some software to either replace them or show them how to do their job. It is not just fear they are experiencing; it is also reasonable for them to feel more than a little bit insulted. If their fear is a reasonable and justified response to our presence, then we need to anticipate it and have a strategy to mitigate it.

Mitigating Fear

The process of mitigating the fear is very similar to the techniques used in change management to overcome resistance. You are looking to involve everyone in the process and demonstrate that the project will improve their job. To do this, it is critical to help them understand that what they know about the job is essential to the data science process, and more importantly it will be ongoing. I have yet to see a model that didn't require regular updating and adjustment as business conditions and requirements change.

Secondly, you need to help them understand that data science solutions are tools, tools that still need to be applied by people. It is extremely

---

[6] M.S. Brown. May 31, 2016. "How To Overcome The 3 Fears That Undermine Data Analytics," Forbes Magazine.

rare that the result of a data science project is a piece of software that completely replaces humans in the process. This is so rare that even though I have met two managers who have explicitly stated this as a goal, neither of them implemented it. Often, the efficiency gains produced by a good data science solution mean that the people doing the jobs can focus on doing better work on the challenging and interesting parts of their job, and perhaps fewer new people need to be hired as the business grows.

Ideally, the process of mitigating fears will take the people you are working with to a state of excitement. You want them to be genuinely interested in the project and invested in its success. One way of achieving these aims is to include questions such as the following in your process:

"Which parts of your job do you find dull?"
"Where do you think the inefficiencies are in your company?"
"Which parts of your job would you like to be automated?"
"What decisions do you have to make where you feel that not enough is known in order to make those decisions?"

All these questions are about helping the operational staff to feel involved. When they focus on thinking about aspects of their job that could be improved, it helps them to envision a version of their job that is more enjoyable than what it currently is. This builds a positive association with the data science process, rather than one of unwelcome invasion into their domain.

Of course, if the project you have been given is very specific then these questions may not be relevant, and you may not be able to ask them in this form. However, you can adapt the questions. For example, if you are charged with improving conversions in an online shop, you might use questions like:

"Which part of the shopping experience do you think is causing the most drop off?"
"How would you test that?"
"What do you think is your biggest blind spot in understanding the needs of your customers?"

In all these questions you are trying to achieve multiple things:

1. Demonstrate to the client that they have valuable knowledge.
2. Encourage them to think abstractly about the kinds of problems in the process that might be solvable through data science.
3. Move the dialogue from prescribing solutions to discussing problems.
4. Get them excited about the possibility that things could be better.

It is worthwhile taking time before an engagement begins to put together some questions that can help you achieve these goals. It is likely that your initial questions won't be exactly right, so be prepared to adapt them. If done correctly, you should be able to take those initial meetings and turn them from a guarded and potentially hostile exchange into one that produces valuable insights and initiates a mutually beneficial exchange.

Managing Multiple Client Levels

In the scenarios I outlined previously, where you need to get operational staff on your side, there is potential for additional problems to emerge. Your services will typically have been retained by a senior manager who wants to improve some aspect of the business. That manager will have asked multiple other people in their organization to work with you. This will usually be a combination of operational staff and junior managers who are familiar with processes involved.

You will be interacting with all these people to get the critical details that help you evaluate the proposed solution. In that exchange you are trying to mitigate their fears and include them in the process. However, if what you learn leads you to propose alternative approaches that are too far from your initial problem statement, you may find that the people who hired you are no longer happy.

This is a difficult path to tread. You need to ensure that your initial line of questioning and strategy reflects what has been asked of you by those who employed you. However, as is often the case, those making the decisions do not always know the particulars of the business processes or data sets particularly well. You will need to judge whether the initial description of the solution or problem makes sense given what the actual business processes are, and what operational staff are telling you.

You may well need to go back to your initial project sponsors with an amendment to the problem, driven by what your engagement has uncovered. There are advantages and disadvantages to doing this. Some managers like to cling to an ideological vision of what their organization does or are intolerant of the idea that they are not experts in their business. It is always possible that you have been employed because they refuse to listen to what their own people tell them. If this is the case the situation may not be resolvable. In general, all you can do in these situations is lay out the facts you have gathered and a clear line of reasoning. It is possible that the staff have not been listened to because they could not communicate their ideas effectively. Give lots of credit for where ideas come from and articulate all the details with clarity and logic. This may be enough to create a more positive dialogue inside your client's organization.

Despite the risk involved with taking this step, you will find that it is an effective strategy to get the operational staff on your side. You have listened to them and managed to get their voices heard above them. They will likely be somewhat disgruntled that it took an outsider to come in before they were heard, but at least you are listening to them. Mitigate the disgruntlement by giving ample credit for the insights that have driven the revised problem definition.

If you decide that you cannot go back to the sponsors and suggest a change to the project, or if you try and fail, then you must make a strategic choice about how to proceed. At this point, you should have collected enough information to evaluate the solution you are being tasked to deliver. If you believe it could succeed but the predominate risk is that the operational staff do not believe in it, then the primary challenge to the project is either convincing them or mitigating their resistance. If, on the other hand, you believe that the solution will fail, then it usually seems like you only have two remaining choices:

1. To implement something that you think will fail.
2. To walk away from the project.

Very few of us are ever in the position of being able to do option 2, which leaves us with the unpalatable nonchoice of implementing something we think will fail. In my experience, the more effort you have put into developing strong communication skills and strategies for building trust with your clients, the less often you will end up in this situation. However, sometimes it is unavoidable, which is why it is good to have mitigation strategies for when it occurs. I have two strategies for this, which I call Salvageable Shipwreck and Informative Denial. I will outline both in more detail, but keep in mind that these strategies are backup plans, not methods of sabotage. You need to make every effort to deliver what the client has asked for. This is true even if you have recommended against it, or silently believe it will fail, perhaps even more so.

Salvageable Shipwreck

Salvageable Shipwreck is a strategy particularly suited to data science projects that are product driven. The client has some specific software, model/algorithm, or dashboard in mind that you believe will not solve their problem. The essential idea behind this strategy is that you look for opportunities to build reusable assets while attempting to deliver the solution you believe is doomed. In doing so, you are formulating a plan to sell the client on an alternative outcome, when and if their desired outcome fails. These reusable assets can be processed data sets, functions, or models that can be applied across a range of potential problems. You will typically need to be more conscientious in how you structure the code so that it is not tied to the specifics of the current project.

In principle, the Salvageable Shipwreck idea should be an underlying strategy in everything you do. We all need to look for reuse opportunities. In this scenario, it becomes vital because if the project's stated goal does in fact fail, you need to have something positive to bring to the client. Which brings us to the second aspect of this strategy: a set of reusable assets may not be sufficient to keep your client happy. Ideally, you should have some idea of how those assets can be immediately reused to deliver value. This means that you should be selective in what is reusable, perfect software engineering is hard and time consuming. When you have limited time available, you should focus your attention on making reusable components from the parts of the current project that can be immediately used in another part of the business.

If it becomes clearer and clearer that the project is failing, then it is ideal to have a project plan, prototype, or demonstration ready. This requires additional work, outside the scope of the current project, but it will make the discussion with sponsors easier. What you want to do is present the following three key points:

1. Outline why the project is not delivering the expected results.
2. Explain the components of the project that can be reused.
3. Outline how these components can be used for an alternative outcome.

Informative Denial

The informative denial strategy is more suitable for projects that tend to be information- or insights-focused. These are situations where you believe that an underlying hypothesis, or assumption, is not valid. The idea is to design the experiments and analytical work you do in order to demonstrate the nature of this falsehood, while simultaneously learning as much as you can about the issues surrounding it. The objective is that when your client realizes that they are wrong there will still be enough additional information in the experimental results to set you on a constructive path.

Ideally, this form of scientific thinking should be a part of any insights-driven project. You should always try and maximize the amount each experiment reduces your uncertainty; however, that requires some agreement on where your uncertainty lies. The key here is that your experiments are restricted by what the client wants investigated, so you need to think of peripheral and closely related questions that are likely to have some value.

A useful strategy is to control for, or simply collect, variables that are informed by your context gathering. This will give you a range of potential insights that relate directly to what the operational staff in the business have been telling you. For example, you may be investigating churn for a Telco sponsor who believes that the problem is related to network congestion. At the same time, operational staff are telling you that there are large numbers of international students and tourists using the services and heavy pricing competition for their business. While you are building a data set that maps patterns of congestion on the network to individual customers and their loyalty, you can collect information about their residency status and scrape competitor pages for insights into competitive behavior. Ultimately, these information sources can lead to strategic insights into how to compete for these customers.

Summary

Achieving buy-in is one of the more difficult aspects of our work. It can be present or absent at different levels of an organization, to differing degrees. Its absence can be driven by a variety of feelings and motivations that are usually disguised and may not even be conscious. However, it can also be absent due to perfectly rational objections to a project.

The level of buy-in you have at different parts of an organization will heavily influence the outcome of your project. A former colleague once reported to me that months of work turned out to be a waste because the operational staff (not the manager who initiated the project) were feeding them rubbish data so that once the project failed, the subordinate in question could turn around and solve the problem. The people you are trying to help can be your greatest hurdle.

To achieve buy-in, we need to focus on including people in the process as we gather information and formulate solutions. This often involves juggling across teams and levels within an organization. It is achieved over iterations, through strong communication strategies, but it is rarely complete. You will need to strategically determine when you have buy-in from enough of the right people for a project to proceed and succeed.

CHAPTER 4

Getting Context

In the preceding chapters we have looked at ways to get a clearer problem definition. Be it through helping the client understand what data science is, moving them away from talking about solutions before the problem is understood, or by managing operational staff who may not be happy about an outsider being brought in to change their processes.

We have spoken about the importance of context multiple times in the discussion so far. It is critical in evaluating solutions that have been proposed, and its collection is one of the ways that we encourage buy-in from operational staff. But we have not yet discussed what context is in detail, and how to determine when you have all the context you will need, that is the goal of this chapter.

When, What, How, and Why

In the process of getting those clear statements of the problem, you should also be looking to gain context of the surrounding business and data collection processes. It is worthwhile building a checklist of everything you need to know. Ideally, this will be a custom checklist based on your understanding of the domain and type of problem. Regardless of the finer details you will almost always need the when, what, and how of the problem. The why is likely to be the thing you are asked to solve, but the client may have some ideas that limit the scope of the project.

The When

The when part of a problem context has multiple critical threads. This will include the timings of all events that occur in a causal chain. In an earlier chapter we discussed an SMS containing recommendations; in the process, we spoke about a series of events that occur in a customer's interaction with support. This is one form of when, not specific times, but the sequences of events: B happens after A but before C. In addition to the fine-grained events that determine the structure and sequence of all business processes, there are also three critical *whens* that exert influence over how you will solve any data science problem.

First, there is the *when* of feedback. When does the organization become aware that the specific event or problem has occurred? Is it much after the event itself, or is it immediate? This issue is likely to affect how the data about the problem is collected and how fresh it is. For example, financial organizations typically do not know that they are writing a bad home loan until years after the loans have been granted. This kind of delay in the feedback means your data can be years out of date, and often necessitates looking for proxy signals with a shorter time horizon. In the financial industry, this means looking at missed payments.

Next, there is the *when* of the required action or intervention. In other words, when does an organization need to act in order to try and solve the problem? If the action needs to take place long before the event you are trying to affect, then the data available will typically be poorer and the problem more difficult to solve. If the action has a shorter time horizon, then you can use much fresher data in your models.

The timing of the action has a subordinate concern, which is: when will the outcome of an intervention be known? This will have consequences if you are looking at solutions that require a sequence of actions. For example, many modern marketing funnels contain a series of messages and offers that are sent to prospects. Typically, these are sent over fixed intervals of time, with the capacity for the user's behavior to influence what is sent. If a more generous offer is sent too soon after the previous offer you can cannibalize your own margins. However, if it is sent too late you run the risk of losing the customer to a competitor.

The final critical issue of timing is knowing when all the data points become available. Typically, you are given data sets divorced from the practical reality of how they are collected and collated. In the real world there are usually multiple business systems involved, each of which introduces delays in the process. Some systems require more data processing than others, that processing is often scheduled in batch runs, which means the differences in availability of data coming from these systems could be measured in days.

The timing of data collection is tightly related to the previous topic of action. If the business is open to the idea of different potential intervention points, then you need to interleave these interventions with consideration of data availability. There will be a trade-off between (1) when you can effectively predict something, (2) when the data will be available to make that prediction, and (3) when the intervention is most likely to be successful. These three *whens* will drive a considerable amount of the design compromises in any data science solution.

The What

The *what* elements of a business process are as multifaceted as the *when*. You need to know enough about what happens at each stage through the whole process that you can understand and evaluate a problem. We spoke previously about the importance of understanding the event sequence, but it is just as critical to know what happens at each point in this sequence. It is difficult to prescribe everything that needs to be known to fully qualify a what. It is worthwhile asking yourself if you completely understand a point in the process before you move on. Even better, as we suggested in an earlier chapter, paraphrase what you have learned in a narrative and let your client correct you or fill in missing details.

There are, however, some data science specific details you will want to ask in every engagement. Ask what data is available that represents the process being described. What are the inputs, internals, and outcomes at each stage of a business process? Finally, what is it that is currently being done to mitigate known problems? Is there an existing data science model? Or is there some manual process that is being used to intervene?

The How

The final chore of this information gathering exercise is to get the answer to a variety of different *how* questions. How do they know there is a problem (in other words, how is it measured)? How do they collect the data they have? All of the *what* questions about data have a corresponding *how* question about the acquisition of that data. Finally, how will they know when the problem is solved. This is a measurement question in disguise, sometimes this phrasing helps get a better answer than when asking directly for current measurement of the problem. If not, it will lead to a very productive and critical discussion about how your work will be evaluated.

Ask for Data

At some point, you will begin to feel that the scope and definition of the problem is taking shape. At this point, you should be asking for data sets that clearly demonstrate the problem. In other words, the data you see should correspond to the *when* and the *what* of every part of the business process that was described to you.

If the data doesn't correspond to what you have been told, then plot it and show your client. It is possible that you have been given the wrong data, it is also possible that the client has misunderstood what is happening inside their own business. You can use the combination of the context you have been given and what you see in the data as a launching point for further discussion and investigation.

Typically, the next stage will involve bringing in people responsible for providing the data as well as those closest to the systems that collect the data. At this juncture, you are trying to identify if the data has been collected without errors, prepared without errors, and represents what the various people involved think it represents.

Be prepared for problems at any stage in this process, the translation from data to business insight can go horribly wrong in some organizations. This problem occurs sometimes because nonnumerical people provide imprecise definitions of what they want measured, or because they have people running reports for them who don't really understand what it is they are asking for. There are a range of reasons why it might occur, the most important thing is that you recognize it, and recognize it early. You do not want to spend time trying to solve a problem that does not exist.

It is also possible that you have misunderstood the problem statement. When you are showing the client plots of their data, and explaining what you see, they might be able to identify your misunderstanding and clarify it for you. Either way, you want to make sure that what the client is saying, what you are understanding, and what the data is saying are all in alignment. This should be the first thing you do with the data.

Early recognition helps you avoid two common disastrous project fates: First, if the client is wrong about the problem and you bring this up later, you will have to explain why you have been spending their money on a nonexistent problem. Secondly, if you misunderstood their statement of the problem, then it saves you struggling to find a solution to the wrong problem and then needing to explain why you have not solved the problem they asked you to solve. The rule of thumb here is to constantly ensure coherence between the data you see and what is being said in meetings about the problem. If you maintain that coherence, then there is an entire family of disastrous project endings you can avoid.

Once you have a data set that clearly demonstrates the problem as it was described to you, then you can look for additional context in the data. A good rule of thumb is to ask the clients about what they think is driving the observed problems and then ask the clients for data sets that contain additional variables that you can use to visualize those relationships. They may not have this data; in which case, you can ask how they came to the ideas and conclusions they hold. You should use the client for their knowledge of the problem space, but you should not take them at their word. People believe all manner of things based on bad (or absent) evidence, and businesspeople and managers are no exception.

By the same token, you should not fall into the habit of dismissing ideas and explanations for which there are no data. Just because they cannot give precise descriptions of how they came to hold certain beliefs or entertain certain hypotheses does not mean they are wrong. The human brain can identify a great many patterns without being consciously aware of how it does it, and although intuition can be error prone it has been shown to be useful for some styles of decision making.[1] You should treat ideas that may lack immediate evidence with consideration until you have reason not to. This does not mean believe everything you are told; it means look for ways to establish whether what you are told agrees with the data you observe.

---

[1] L. Kutsch. August 15, 2019. "Can We Rely on Our Intuition?," *Scientific American.*

As an example of this, consider another customer retention scenario. You can ask the client for a data set that shows when customers are acquired and when their last purchase is. Ask them for their definition of what churn is: it might be that three months goes by without a purchase, or it might be that the volume of transactions decreases. You want to understand how they have identified the problem in the data, so you can look at alternative definitions and understand what the actual change in behavior is. The client might have hypotheses about the problem being driven by the responsiveness of their website, or limitations in inventory. Both things are measurable and should exist in data sets somewhere.

Issues With Data

At the same time as you are investigating the data for coherence with the problem statement, you should also be investigating potential problems with the data. All your context gathering questions up to this point should have given you a sense of the data gathering process. It is worthwhile to test whether the data presented conforms to this. For example, if you are told that the data is logged once a customer logs into the website, and the churn event is initiated by a form lodgement on the website, then you should find data about the web session preceding each churn event. The congruence between the problem description and the data should be reflected in numbers or frequencies of events. It should be in the ratios or relationships between things, it should be in the cardinality of categorical variables and in the range of numeric variables.

In addition, you should be on the lookout for inherent problems in the data gathering process. Not just that the data appears to have been collected in the way it was described, but that there are no consistent biases or flaws in this process. As an example, I was once given data about the conversion of sales opportunities related to digital media for advertising placements. The goal of which was to try and understand the advertising demand across verticals and industry segments the company was over and underperforming in. Further investigation revealed that the process by which an "opportunity" was logged, was arbitrary and at the discretion of the sales representative. The savvy reps understood that it was in their interest to hold off entering data until the sale looked likely to close. This improved their conversion rate, and as long as the sales funnel was reasonably well populated, they looked comparatively better than their peers. Sales reps are not randomly assigned to accounts, which meant that there was biased sampling of the market in that data set. It did not accurately reflect what the real demand for media looked like.

This example demonstrates that a single flawed point in the data collection process can undermine its quality or utility. You need to keep asking questions about how data is generated to understand if it really reflects the system you want to understand. Understandably, there are limitations to what you can uncover through questioning or visualization. Thankfully, with all the attention on bias in machine learning there are now algorithmic approaches you can take to try and identify problems in the data. For example, you can build models that try and identify the source of data from a record, which can be used to determine if there are systemic problems in amalgamated data sets.[2]

Context Without Data

In some cases, your client may not have data sitting around ready to analyze, or they may not know where to start with collecting data. This situation heightens the importance of getting detailed contextual information. If they are asking for solutions to a very general problem statement, then you can start by asking for a story style description of how the problem occurs. For example, when investigating customer churn, you might start asking questions like:

"How do you acquire your customers?"
"Do they tend to stick with one type of product?"
"What kind of communications do you use to keep them engaged? E-mail, website pop-ups, phone calls?"
"Do you currently have a way of recognising a customer that might churn?"
"What actions do you take?"

---

[2]   S. Biderman, and W. Scheirer. November 2020. "Pitfalls in Machine Learning Research: Reexamining the Development Cycle," *NeuroIPS Workshop*.

As discussed previously, the narrative style helps people remember the relevant facts and notice what is missing. You will need to selectively choose when to dive in and get sufficient detail to build a causal map of the sequence of events. At the same time, you should be thinking about what data might be available, asking what systems are used at each stage, who operates those systems, and whether they produce log files.

As you build up the narrative and dive into details you will identify gaps in their knowledge, which may require additional people in future meetings. All the while you should be imagining what data might be collected and what patterns would be present, if the business problem is as it has been described to you.

The end state of this interview process should be a mental model of the business process, which will inform you whether the client's problems are genuine. You should see this through the facts of the causal map and the logical sequence of events. You should also have a sense of what the existing data sets are that could be brought together to try and solve their problem.

Summary

Sufficient context is critical for understanding the nature, and limitations, of both the business problem and the data related to it. It will help you evaluate proposed solutions, and it may even help you identify nonproblems: problems that are either nonexistent or so small that addressing them is not cost effective. Context will help you sculpt any potential interventions and help build the case for the use of a particular intervention, given what you know about the timing of feedback and data collection.

Questions about existing processes surrounding the problem are particularly important. They will help you identify potential biases in the data you see, and they help you understand how any solution you provide will be implemented and interact with other systems. You need to ensure that once you understand the problem, you can see it reflected clearly in the data. Show plots to the client and be certain that you are seeing the same problem they are. Be certain that you completely understand the way the data is collected. Be certain that the data reflects a real business problem, and not something unusual about the data collection process.

CHAPTER 5

Getting Measurements

In the last chapter we discussed the progression from gathering contextual descriptions of the problem, through to data sets that demonstrate it. We placed particular emphasis on ensuring that you have coherence between the descriptions you are given and what you see in the data. Evaluating whether the data reflects what you have been told will have started you down the path of this chapter, where we focus on getting a concise answer to the key question:

"How do you measure the state of the problem?"

If the problem statement is itself clear, then the answer to this question should be almost self-evident. This is not always the case, sometimes measurement occurs through proxy signals or involves multiple assumptions and stages of reasoning. If we consider a customer churn example, the company may not have a current metric for retention. It may be a casual observation that has been made by multiple people in the organization that has prompted the project. The informal nature of this impetus is not necessarily a problem, but it does mean that you should be wary of starting the project before there is some form of robust metric in place. If the evaluation of your project success depends on casual observations, you can be in a precarious position.

You need to get agreement on some form of precise and unambiguous measurement of the state of the problem before you begin work. This is not just for the sake of evaluation of what you do, but so that you have data against which to test hypotheses and use in your analysis.

It is worth noting that when you start talking about measurement, some organizations will refer you to their standardized methodology for generating business metrics. The balanced scorecard (BSC) is a popular and widely adopted system.[1] This is typically not the kind of measurement we are looking for in a data science use case. The BSC and other similar methodologies involve very high-level metrics for overall business performance that are typically not collected with the kind of granularity we need in data science. Why does the granularity matter? It matters because in data science our metrics are used as a method of understanding what drives outcomes in the specific business process. We typically need fine granularity so that we have sufficient data points to measure, or model, the relationships across the properties, actions, and outcomes in a business process. Standard business metric systems are generally about measuring if some program had an impact at a macroscopic level, for the purpose of saying if it was successful. Not *why* it was successful.

In this chapter, I will discuss three different types of metrics that are commonly used in data science projects: built-in or predetermined metrics, inferable metrics, and proxy signals. The situations in which they are used, and their limitations will be discussed.

Built-In Metrics

The ideal scenario is one in which the data science problem itself is defined in terms of a metric. For example, the client might say that the average customer lifetime (first to last purchase) is less than 12 months, and they want to increase it to 18 months. This is an ideal situation, you have an explicit statement of the status quo, how it is measured, and what the goal state is.

Note that a phrase like average customer lifespan is not self-evident. It needs to be qualified by how the start point and the end point are measured. In this example, you probably also require some definition of when the customer is considered churned, is it 6 or 12 months after the customer's last purchase? What happens if a customer returns after 12 months? Are they then considered a new customer? Or are they added back to the original customer record? If the latter is the case, then it will create a skew

---

[1] A. Van Looy, and A. Shafagatova. 2016. "Business Process Performance Measurement: A Structured Literature Review of Indicators, Measures and Metrics," *SpringerPlus* 5, p. 1797. https://doi.org/10.1186/s40064-016-3498-1

in the data of potentially long-term customers with lower-than-average purchase activity. It is critical to understand the edge cases of any system of measurement so you consider how it might influence your analysis.

Inferable Metrics

More than likely the problem will not be stated with an explicit metric but may easily lend itself to potential metrics. For example, a business might be struggling with the fact that their costs are scaling poorly with their revenue, and hence they are unable to increase profitability. You can start by looking at the changes in their costs per unit of production. Examining this and looking at its historical trend will verify the existence of the problem. It may even serve as a baseline against which success is judged.

The key here is to take the problem statement and determine a way that it could be measured from the available data. Once you have a measure that verifies the problem, you can start to talk about goals for the project and their feasibility. Alternatively, you could try and refine the metric to refine the scope of the project.

For example, continuing with our scaling problem, you might want to look at the relationship between the production costs with various factors that capture how the company has been scaling. This could be the unit costs against the number of employees, or unit costs in relation to the square meters of shop floor, or number of machines, and so on. All such efforts may result in a more refined definition of the problem. For example, how do you stop the unit cost of production increasing with the number of employees.

In the process of refining the scope in this way you may discover inescapable limits. Perhaps some dimensions of the business scaling are intrinsically linked with the output. The act of scope refinement will help you eliminate dimensions that cannot be improved on. There is a danger that the process of analyzing and refining the scope of the problem will result in a realization that the problem is either unsolvable or trivial. This should be an acceptable outcome for a data science process. Part of the attraction of data scientists to many businesses managers is our ability to cast an impartial eye over a business process and draw rational conclusions about whether there are feasible pathways for improvement.

Proxy Signals

The most difficult cases are when the problem description is not immediately associated with any data that is being collected that could be considered a metric. There are only two options in this situation. You can request that the business starts to collect a specific data signal and wait for it to be sufficient. If this is not feasible or desirable (given time constraints), then you need investigate what could be used as a proxy measurement.

A proxy measurement involves deciding on something that you can measure, where you have good reasons to expect it to be tightly coupled or correlated with what you would want to measure. We previously used the example of missed payments being used in the financial services industry as a proxy signal for loan defaults. They necessarily precede a default, and although not every missed payment will result in a default, it does allow the tracking of changes in behavior that might be an early warning indication of coming defaults.

With any proxy signal you need to get your client to agree that the proxy is an acceptable way to approximately measure the phenomenon they care about. You need to get their agreement that you will use the proxy in your analysis, and that the results of your work will be evaluated (at least initially) by the proxy signal. Do not rush over this point; it is reasonable for a business manager to assume that the focus on the proxy is just an initial stage. You need to make sure that they understand that direct measurement of the problem can only be achieved with investment and patience while that data is collected.

A common example of this kind of problem comes from clients who want to solve a real, or imagined, problem with brand reputation. They may have data in the form of a survey (supplied by a brand consultant), and you may find that this survey was a one-off event, too expensive to repeat, and done with a disappointingly low sample size.

You need to begin discussions about how to create an alternative, repeatable measurement. One that is either a better indication of what management cares about, or at least closely related and important. The place to start is with effects, ask the client what effects they believe a change in brand reputation has. Ask them what kind of time scales are required to observe the effects of these changes in reputation. This might allow you to identify multiple potential proxy signals that you can investigate. Depending on which of them have readily available data, you can make recommendations as to how they might use data to track their brand reputation.

Summary

You should aim to never start an engagement without getting agreement on how the problem will be measured for the sake of the project. This measurement will inform your analysis and will be the yardstick against which your work is judged. Having an explicit metric allows you to benchmark where the existing systems or processes are operating before you even begin, and thereby monitor your progress. It is not only critical to helping you succeed; it also helps you demonstrate what you have achieved and avoid many of the potential problems associated with ill-defined problems before the project starts.

CHAPTER 6

Consider Interventions

In the preceding chapters, we discussed getting a solid understanding of the context surrounding the problem and how it is measured. As you gain an understanding of this context you will start to see potential points for intervention. In other words, ways in which your work could be used to make decisions or take actions that will influence the outcomes of the business process.

Once you understand the data that is available you will begin to see the contact points where data-driven interventions are possible. Despite the hype around the possibilities of big data, it is quite common for the potential intervention points to be very limited in number. Typically, these intervention points are defined by a combination of when the critical data becomes available and when the mechanical requirements of the intervention are aligned. This could be driven by direct contact with a customer, or the availability of data to internal teams. In this chapter, we will discuss identifying the actors, systems, and situations that will be involved in an intervention. Followed by the design of the action and intervention itself.

Why Now?

It may seem premature to discuss potential interventions before the project begins. If the project is entirely exploratory with no particular expectations on the outcome, then this might be true. However, I would suggest that it is worthwhile going through a process to identify how your analysis could affect the real-world systems because it can help reduce the scope of the project.

One reason is that it may limit the kinds of models or analytical work you do. There is no point providing a model that requires information that will not be available at the point in time when action needs to be taken. Synchronizing actions with the timing of data and events is often the most critical component of deploying models. Just because you can predict something in advance, does not mean that you can affect it. You need to consider the balance between the ability to analyze or predict something, versus the time horizon that is available to affect it.

In order to identify the potential points of intervention in an existing process there are multiple key pieces of information you will need. The first thing is to understand if the point of action is likely to be equivalent to the moment at which the problem is recorded. In some data science use cases these points are equivalent. Take, for example, a document classification use case in which you are trying to improve the efficiency of a process that depends on the content or type of document. The document classifier is inserted into the system to route documents to the right systems or teams. There is no ambiguity in this case. The problem (inefficient routing of documents) has an associated action that is inserted at exactly the moment at which the inefficiency makes itself apparent (the start of processing).

In many other data science use cases, the point of action will be very different to the point of problem measurement. Customer churn, predictive maintenance, human resource forecasting, and indeed most predictive problems all require taking action in advance of the event being predicted. Other use cases, like root cause analysis, and optimization require wholistic solutions achieved by posthoc analysis, rather than point-in-time actions.

Your first job is to identify the overall category of action that will be taken: same time point, preceding time point, or wholistic system change. Once this is done, there is a process much like context gathering in which you tease out the dimensions and limitations of the potential actions.

Identify the Actors

The actors are the people who will need to change their behavior for a given intervention to be implemented. The key question to answer here is: "Who are the people who are working in the business process who have a direct ability to impact the problematic outcome?" In other words, which employees have sufficient contribution to the outcome that a change in behavior could mechanically impact the result.

In some cases, the problem may involve entirely automated systems. However, even in these limited cases there will be people who design, maintain, and monitor these systems. In addition, there will be people who deal with the outputs of these systems and oversee the downstream affects. It is worthwhile uncovering all the people whose job would be directly affected by anything you deliver.

There may or may not be an obvious line of questioning to get this information. For example, when we previously spoke about customer satisfaction with a support system, someone might argue that the people at the coal face of the problem are the customers. After all, it is their dissatisfaction that we are looking to change. While that is strictly speaking true, we are typically not able to directly control the customer's thoughts. Instead, we need to think about the people who will carry the burden of implementing any changes we propose. This may mean it is the behavior of the support staff themselves.

Alternatively, the customer dissatisfaction may originate earlier and be related to interaction with some other part of the organization. There may be multiple competing hypotheses about the origination points for the customer dissatisfaction. It is worthwhile trying to enumerate these and explicitly call out the subset that your investigation will be able to address.

To take another example, we also previously discussed lead generation use cases, in which a model is used to rank prospective customers by their likelihood to convert. We might say that although this also touches the customer, it is really the salespeople whose behavior would change when solving the problem, because they would be choosing customers to contact based on their lead score ranking. Alternatively, if it turned out that the models indicated an important match between the sales staff and the prospective customer, then the intervention might be a system that allocates accounts to sales staff in order to maximize conversions.

It is important to note that you are not deciding at this point where the intervention will occur. That will likely be a decision to make once some analysis has been done. The idea at this stage is to have some sense of where these potential touch points may be, so that your analysis can be conducted in a way that helps inform that decision.

In summary, this stage of questioning is all about getting context on the potential touch points, whether they are human, automated, or wholistic structural changes. We want to get a sense of what actions might need to be taken to solve the problem. Simply engaging management in thinking about this is likely to help them realize that the problem may be more complicated than previously thought. It may prompt them to begin thinking about the human-oriented difficulties of putting a solution in place.

Identify the Systems

We mentioned in the previous section that sometimes, due to automated processes, human beings are not directly involved at the moment where intervention occurs. Instead, some kind of system has the responsibility of carrying out the intended action. Regardless of whether the process is automated or entirely manual, there will always be a system, or set of systems, you will need to consider when implementing your solution. These include the systems that collect, transform, and assemble data. As well as the systems that employees use to enter, modify, or inspect data. Finally, any systems that are responsible for interaction with customers or products to deliver outcomes.

Understanding what all these systems are, who uses them, and the variety of limitations they have is critical to scoping the potential interventions. The limitations of these systems can take a variety of forms. We have already mentioned some of these in the preceding discussion, but here is a summary of the key dimensions to consider:

1. Availability. When do the systems make the data available? (Relative to the events that the data relates to). In other words, how long after something happens will there be data that can be used in a decision?
2. Volumes. Are there limitations to the volumes of data? These can be limitations in how the data is collected, or limitations in the storage and processing. The impact of these kinds of limitations have lessened as technology has progressed, nevertheless they usually still exist.

3. Actions. Are there inherent limitations on the actions that a system can take? If you are looking for automated actions or responses, then whatever system that delivers these will have limitations. This can be Application Programming Interface (API) throughputs, message sizes, and so on.

4. Interactions. If there are multiple systems involved, then you need to understand the limitations on communication between systems. Again, this could be regarding API functionality, or fundamental differences in how data about events are represented.

5. Barriers. Are there barriers between these systems? These can be network barriers, data custody barriers, cultural or political limitations to what can be achieved.

6. Ownership. Who has ownership of these systems? In other words, who will need to sign off on any changes that will need to be made? Once you know who these people are, you need to know if they are engaged in the project. If you have never met them, ask to meet them. If you anticipate making changes to their systems, then you need to start building trust as early as possible.

When you understand these limitations, you may be able to rule out certain potential interventions that would be in-principle possible. At the very least you will find that by identifying the limitations you will help your client understand potential dependencies in the project. For example, it might become apparent that in order to implement the desired intervention they will need to upgrade or replace a key system. Earlier identification of any dependencies like these will help with project delivery and maintaining timelines.

Identify the Situations

Once you have identified the crucial people and systems that are involved in the points of contact with your problem, you need to understand the standard way that events unfold. In all likelihood most of these details would have been answered in the process of gathering your problem context, but there is a chance the details are missing. It is entirely possible that the context of the original problem statement may be very different from the context of the potential intervention. This is usually due to a time separation. You might have gathered ample context about the process by which a customer churns, but if the intervention point is three months prior to that, then you will need to collect the context surrounding the intervention as well.

Asking about what happens when a customer calls for support might have helped identify issues like the one raised in a previous chapter; that the customers all choose to speak to an operator on the phone at the first available opportunity. The issue we discussed here was that the customers never got to the point where the chosen intervention could help them. We want to uncover these facts before the project begins.

Sometimes, when we ask questions about these details, the stakeholders may not know the answers. It is not unreasonable to request reports, statistics, or an introduction to people in the organization who understand the process more thoroughly. Postponing the project start for the sake of several rounds of information gathering can help you avoid many of the problems we are discussing. Resist the temptation to jump in and start your analysis, or build a model or a system, until you understand the existing systems and the ways in which people interact with them. A high-level understanding is often sufficient, but it is required to build effective data science systems.

One of the ways the nature of systems influence intervention is through the degree to which an intervention can be adaptive. In some situations, we choose to use a fixed one-size-fits-all approach, in which all customers receive the same intervention if they are identified as being in need. Increasingly, many disciplines recognize the value of individualized interventions that adapt to the scenario. The intervention can be adaptive across different individuals through the use of so-called tailoring variables. This approach is known as personalization in marketing and individualization in medical practice. Alternatively, the intervention can be adaptive across time, in the sense that the action is adjusted with respect to the history of interactions with the customer.[1]

---

[1] I. Nahum-Shani, M. Qian, D. Almirall, W.E. Pelham, B. Gnagy, G. Fabiano, J. Waxmonsky, J. Yu, and S. Murphy. 2012. "Experimental Design and Primary Data Analysis Methods for Comparing Adaptive Interventions," *Psychological Methods* 17, no. 4, pp. 457–477.

Most organizational systems will have limitations in the degree to which interventions can be individualized. A thorough investigation of these limits will help you determine if certain interventions are feasible and allow you to focus on approaches that are genuinely actionable.

Identify the Actions

The final category of information gathering relates to the specific actions to be taken. At this point, we understand the people and systems involved. We understand the context in which the problem occurs and the events that surround the potential intervention point. The final question we want to answer is:

> "What range of actions can we consider taking in order to solve the problem?"

It is important to note that many clients will have some ideas about these actions, but it is unlikely that they have thoroughly investigated all possible interventions. The initial answers you get to this line of questioning will be heavily informed by current expectations, existing or previous approaches, and the experiences of all stakeholders in similar projects.

It is critical to qualify whether each and every action has been previously tried and what the results were. If the actions are novel for the organization, then it is worthwhile understanding where the idea came from. If the project is being solution driven (as discussed previously), the action may already have been defined. Use this exercise to understand the reasoning that led to that action being chosen. You can phrase this in a way that indicates you are trying to understand the scope of actions that could be taken to solve a problem, and why they were ruled out.

This discussion need not necessarily focus on very specific actions. Investigating types or families of action is almost as productive. For example, can we ask whether some form of product customization could be offered? (Price discounts, optional features.) We can ask what kind of outreach is possible? Phone calls, e-mail, SMS, or onsite visit. Can there be internal business process actions taken? These might be application rejections, changes to orders, internal reviews, or upgrades.

It is not impossible that you will encounter a project where the central problem has no known potential action that could feasibly solve the problem. This might occur because the client doesn't know how the business problem is occurring. In which case, the project focus needs to pivot toward generating business insights. If this is the case, you will want to make this change explicit upfront. Emphasize that you will be generating the insights to help them understand the nature of the problem, not solving it. Make it clear to your client that additional work will need to be done to solve the problem. Note, that after exploratory work you may conclude that data science is not required to solve it.

Scoping the space of actions is not just about defining potential approaches to intervene and achieve a solution, it is also about identifying potential roadblocks. A common situation is that there is a wide range of potential actions that could be taken; however, the project sponsors who have engaged you have a limited ability in what they can authorize and deliver. For example, you might discover in the customer support use case the potential actions cover modification of the website content and organization, changing an automated phone systems and retraining of human support operators. However, the scope of the project does not allow for retraining of the staff.

There are a diverse range of organization structures, many of which contain intertwined or isolated domains of responsibility. The various divisions may not play nicely together or may not have the funds available for wide-ranging projects. For these reasons, it is important to understand the limitations of potential actions.

You may be tempted to try and influence the limitations as they have been stated. It is important to be realistic about your ability to influence an organization to make changes that they have told you, are not possible. You can make additional recommendations, but do not forget that a project needs to be delivered, and however irrational the organization of the company might seem to you, you have neither all the context to evaluate it nor the responsibility to. If you can do good work with what you have been given, then perhaps in the next engagement they will consider your more far-reaching and ambitious ideas.

Intervention Design

With a well-scoped-out list of the people, systems, situations, and potential actions, you will be able to quickly identify what the most likely interventions could be. The combination of the four tend to whittle the list of options down and suggest natural touch points. You will need to consider how all four elements combine in a wholistic fashion. You are typically looking for interventions that have the following qualities:

1. Have an intuitive mechanistic relationship with the problem that they are solving.
2. Can be implemented at a point in time that will allow that effect to be felt.
3. Use data that will be provided by the relevant systems at the required point in time.
4. That involve people who are prepared and capable to make the required changes.
5. That are cost effective relevant to the importance of the problem being solved.

The set of actions that satisfy these criteria are typically small. Once you have identified them, you will be able to arrange your analysis and modeling in such a way that results, and conclusions, can lead to a natural recommendation as to which of them is likely to be most effective.

Summary

Considering the space of possible interventions is worthwhile once you have developed an independent understanding of the business problem. The intervention space is constrained by the people and systems involved and must meet the requirements of the situations in which viable actions could be taken. A thorough understanding of the intervention space will allow you to focus your data science project on analysis that will be actionable and effective.

CHAPTER 7

Dwell on Constraints

In the preceding chapters, we have regularly discussed the presence of different kinds of limitations and boundaries to a project. In the previous chapter we discussed system constraints that affect the potential interventions. Limitations could also take the form of organizational constraints that affect the parts of the process that are open to change within the bounds of your project. Regardless of where they occur, limitations are critical to understand thoroughly because they define the space of solutions in which you must operate. As Eugene Yan describes it, there is liberation in a complete understanding of the constraints. You are free to apply any solution that meets them.[1]

Some of the material in this chapter will reiterate and build on points raised previously. This is being done deliberately for didactic emphasis. The core idea is that a thorough understanding of the constraints on your project will help you efficiently and effectively find a solution.

Limitations can emerge at almost any point of the project life cycle. It is worth emphasizing that although the recommendation is to undertake this investigation early in the process, you should keep an eye out for new constraints at any point in the process. Elad Cohen recommends a process of continuously probing for constraints through what-if sessions, in which each development is used as an opportunity to propose scenarios and solutions that might unearth new constraints.[2] In this chapter, we

---

[1] E. Yan. June 2020. "What I Do Before a Data Science Project to Ensure Success," *Blog Post.* https://eugeneyan.com/writing/what-i-do-before-a-data-science-project-to-ensure-success/

[2] E. Cohen. March 22, 2021. "Avoiding the 4 Major Pitfalls of Data Science Projects," *Towards Data Science Blog.* https://towardsdatascience.com/avoiding-the-4-major-pitfalls-of-data-science-projects-8132b295bcdb

will discuss common themes in technical, regulatory, and operational constraints that emerge in data science.

Technical Limitations

We have previously discussed technical limitations in terms of the limits to actions that are permitted within systems that interact directly with customers. We also spoke about limitations derived from the granularity of data collection, and the time required to process it and make it available for analytical purposes.

There are a range of additional technical constraints it is important to be aware of. First, there can be constraints on how your solution is itself deployed. Will it be able to run as an independent application behind an API or will it be integrated directly into some other system? Many systems have limited support for API integration. This constraint will lessen over time, but there will always be some limitations—be that the type of APIs supported, or the throughput they can handle.

The deployment question will bring with it a range of related constraints. For example: How should user access be controlled? Are there firewalls or any other networking restrictions to worry about? Are there restrictions to the hardware and software upon which your solution will run? Are there latency restrictions that will govern how much time your solution will have to execute? Are there preferred application architecture approaches, like the use of microservices?

At the time of writing, there is a widespread adoption of cloud computing technologies. Many organizations are devising strategies for migrating systems from on-premises data centers to cloud-based systems. Some of those cloud-based systems are simply copies of existing legacy systems, others are migrations to open-source solutions, yet others are new proprietary systems released by cloud vendors. At the same time, organizations are adopting new forms of software solutions, like stream processing or Internet of Things (IoT) devices. In addition, they are exploring new forms of computing that have been enabled by the cloud, the so-called serverless architectures. The sheer volume of these new technologies and approaches mean that it is very unlikely that organizations have settled on an end-state solution. In all likelihood, throughout your career, you will continue to see the idea of an ideal software solution evolve and change.

Some organizations attempt to manage that change through policy and procedure. For example, a bank I worked with previously used the idea of a *Reference Architecture* to guide decision making on project implementations. The reference architecture did not describe existing bank systems, but the goal state for the systems. In large traditional businesses that are dealing with an array of legacy systems, they need to manage the evolution of the complexity of these systems. The reference architecture is one such way, it paints a picture of best practices and target state that can help them improve gradually without a monolithic change project.[3]

You would not find a concept like a reference architecture used within a start-up, which is desperately trying to build something that works. But a bank has a very different suite of problems to a tech start-up. This means you need to adjust the kinds of limitations you look for in relation to the kind of organization you are working for. The presence of a reference architecture could be critical for your data science projects, because it could prevent you implementing a solution that may be feasible and meet all other constraints. Your approach would be blocked simply because the solution uses a technology or approach that is being phased out.

Regulatory Limitations

Limitations to your modeling and analysis can extend beyond the mere technical requirements of the systems on which they run. There may be regulatory limitations on the kinds of data that can be used. This has been a common situation in risk modeling for finance but is increasingly considered across other industries. Government organizations are set up to impose these regulatory restrictions to ensure equitable access to resources, such as finance. As such, the use of gender or ethnicity (or proxies thereof) will be excluded from modeling efforts. These regulations

---

[3] R. Cloutier, G. Muller, D. Verma, R. Nilchiani, E. Hole, and M. Bone. January 2009. "The Concept of Reference Architectures," *Systems Engineering* 13, no. 1. https://doi.org/10.1002/sys.20129

may extend to the kinds of interventions you use, or the frequency or content of the offers you make. Other regulations will relate to the data that can be collected, how and where it is stored, and the uses it can be put to. You will need to ask about these kinds of restrictions very directly. If possible, go through some specific categories for which these limitations might apply. For example:

"Are there data sources that we cannot use?"
"Are there limits to the data we can track?"
"What infrastructure can we deploy on?"
"Is this project affected by data residency laws?"
"What privacy legislation impacts this project?"

Unlike the other constraints discussed in this section, the regulatory constraints tend to be beyond modification. This is not to say that they will not change over time, but that the changes that occur will most likely be out of your control and beyond the scope of your project.

Operational Limitations

There are a broad range of constraints on a project that are related to the processes used by the organization. You can think of these as overall limits in the way that a line of business functions. For example, there are hard limits to the number of units a factory can produce, determined by access to raw materials, machinery, and labor. There are limitations to the number of loans a financial institution can underwrite based on their access to capital. In both instances the limits can be changed, but it takes planning and time. The amount of planning and time will vary between industries, so part of your due diligence will be to understand the flexibility in the constraints on the business process. Sometimes changes to these constraints will be on the table as potential interventions, other times they will be explicitly ruled out.

Getting an understanding of these operational limitations consists in understanding the inputs and outputs to the process, and the limiting quantity for each stage of the process. Typically, every stage of any process will have some critical component that limits the rate at which that process can produce results. Relative to all other inputs, it will be the scarcest, or least accessible asset. Your core task is to map out these limiting assets within each stage of the business process.

Flexible Constraints

Not all the constraints you encounter will be fixed. Technical and operational constraints can be open to modification. Some of the constraints will already be subject to plans for modification. Other types of constraints will be completely beyond modification. Understanding the flexibility of the constraints, and any plans for modifications is just as critical as understanding the constraint landscape. Sometimes you may be able to anchor your project to existing plans for operational changes.

If there have been previous data science projects on the same, or similar, problems then speaking with those involved can be a rapid way of understanding any of these constraints. You can save yourself a great deal of pain by picking up from the limitations that have already been discovered through trial and error.

Summary

A thorough understanding of the constraints on your project is critical to effective delivery. The constraints will define the space in which your analysis will be developed and deployed; early understanding of these limitations help you focus on practical solutions. Constraints can exist in the form of technologies, regulations, and operational processes. You should probe and test to determine the hardness of the constraints, because they can change over time, and change may improve your solution. It is recommended that you continuously probe for emerging constraints as your project progresses.

CHAPTER 8

Project Focus

Preceding chapters have guided you through a range of considerations and lines of questioning designed to help you understand the nature of the problem you are trying to solve. This involved getting the client to rewind, to give you the complete problem context, and to outline the constraints your project will operate within.

You will have started looking at data and metrics that give you a robust sense of the reality of the problem that has been posed. With all these pieces in place you are now in a position to determine the specific focus for the project itself. In many scenarios, the project focus will be self-evident. In those instances, this chapter will be a progress check, to determine whether you have that focus, and whether it needs refinement. In other cases, this chapter will be about working with the client to turn the existing problem definition, into a project plan.

Problems Without Projects

In some engagements you can find yourself with a well-defined problem space, but uncertainty about the specific project to be undertaken. If you find yourself in this situation, then it is likely that the questioning process has given you an understanding of one or more very difficult problems that could consist of multiple contributing factors, large amounts of uncertainty and conflicting constraints. You may be struggling to focus in on what approaches you could use to even begin to develop a solution, let alone what it might look like. This might be, in part, due to your inability to imagine how you could address all facets of the problem at once.

This situation occurs naturally when you are tasked with solving a problem that is a large-scale system wide issue with a business. For example, consider an online business that is facing issues with the profitability of customers. The business has different acquisition costs for customers associated with multiple marketing and outreach channels. They have a range of different subsets of services that customers use, on different technology platforms, over different periods of time, that have been gradually changing as their technology develops. There are many different potential sources of the problem, and many potential intervention points from acquisition, app design, product and service structure, or pricing.

The focus for this chapter is how to take what you know about a complicated situation like this and extract a project that consists of a finite solvable part of a multifaceted complicated problem. This chapter is fundamentally about developing, assessing, and comparing the feasibility of multiple potential projects. You should keep in mind that the various different aspects we evaluate—feasibility, Return on Investment (ROI), risk, etc—should be evaluated in parallel.

Divide and Conquer

A key strategy for gaining traction on complicated problems is to identify some part of the entire problem that appears to be solvable in isolation. To do this, you need to map out the degrees of dependence between the various aspects of what has been described to you. Then you can analyze these components for a subset that appears isolated from the full complexity.

For example, a problem like customer churn can, in principle, involve many different touch points in a customer's history with an organization. The various parts of the organization will have hypotheses about what drives positive and negative experiences for customers, as well as how those interactions have flow on effects downstream. You are looking for a part of this sequence that has minimal expected flow on effects, where the impact on the customer appears isolated to that one interaction. For example, an inbound phone call for support is relatively isolated in that it is typically either resolved or not in the single session, and there are often immediate feedback signals such as survey responses or immediate customer behavior. By contrast, an outbound call to verify an identity as part of an application process is only a single component of a longer process, and thereby harder to isolate its impact. The isolation difference in this example is both mechanical (the inbound call is a single customer interaction designed to solve a specific problem) and measurable (there are data points about that interaction that are only about the interaction).

If you are not able to identify any part of the problem that has some natural isolation from the multiple other contributors, then you can turn to an alternative strategy: isolate through subpopulations. In this approach, you are looking to consider all the types of entities that run through process being considered, be they customers, products, or employees. You are looking for criteria that distinguish natural subpopulations of these that allow them to be addressed in isolation. This could be done by many potential features, by geographic region, product type, product features, subscription level, and so on.

In the process of identifying a subpopulation for your project, you could try and identify a subpopulation that is not subject to the entire complexity of the problem. There may be certain factors that are simply excluded because of the characteristics of the subpopulation. For example, in some geographic regions the subscription or pricing model could be different, or the customers may not have been exposed to all products, or certain competitors are absent. You could partition based on the product type because some products lack, or have, certain features that make the problem simpler.

An alternative strategy is to segment by some factor (geography, product) that delineates a more severe version of the problem. Large effect sizes are often easier to influence and can come with a larger pay-off, simply because the return is often related to the size of the impact you can deliver. The trade-off here is between the size of the population that is affected, the difficulty of the problem, and the size of the effect on that subpopulation. The end goal of this process is that segregation of a problem into a subpopulation gives you a problem that is more tractable, and a project that is more feasible.

Feasibility and Priority

If more than one problem, or subproblem, has emerged by this stage in your project you will need to prioritize for the sake of project focus. To do so you want to engage the client in a discussion about the potential impacts of solving those problems individually, or even solving just part of a problem. Most businesses have revenue that is distributed unevenly across a range of sources. You want to understand that distribution so that you can understand which solutions are likely to drive a bigger impact. In principle, the analysis of where the largest business impacts are should have occurred before you are engaged for a project. But you cannot assume that this has happened. It is entirely possible that the client is learning about the fine details of these problems as they discuss them with you.

You may encounter resistance when asking about revenue distribution. Business owners and sponsors can be understandably sensitive about answering questions regarding how much revenue comes from each of their different business units. This will depend on your relationship with the business. If you are an internal data scientist it should be straightforward. It will be more difficult if you are an external consultant, and especially difficult if you are from a boutique consultancy or a lone operator.

There are multiple strategies for mitigating a reluctance to share information about revenue. You can request the information in proportions rather than absolutes. For example, the revenue of unit A is twice that of unit B, but it is one-third that of unit C. It will also seem less invasive if you have already reduced the scope of potential projects, so that questions about revenue are limited to just those business units that are potential targets for the data science project.

An alternative approach to obtaining this information is to frame the inquiry as questions about the expected impact. For example, you ask for the expected percentage effect on the overall company revenue of fixing the problem for business unit A versus B, or process X versus Z. The goal with strategy is to make it entirely transparent that your purpose is not to collect information on the organization's revenue stream, but to determine the project with the most potential impact.

A standard approach to estimating potential impact of a project is a top-down ROI estimate. This begins with an estimate of what the best possible outcome could be; in other words, what is the theoretical best you could do. For example, a transaction system that accepts no fraud, or a maintenance schedule that addresses all machines before they break. You estimate the financial impact of achieving this ideal, then estimate what percentage of this ideal is achievable. For example we can get

20 percent of the potential gains with a six-month project. This process is highly subjective, it assumes that there is some logic to talking about partial progress and that returns are linearly related to that progress. You should feel free to call out these assumptions and use an alternative approach if they are not valid. However, this general process is widely used, and it is often the only way to get an initial estimate for the purposes of prioritization.

The approach described in the previous paragraph can be supplemented with additional detail when it is known. For example, do you know what each instance of fraud/churn/breakage costs the company? How many times do these events occur in a given period of time? What is a reasonable estimate of the cost of intervention? These fundamental figures allow a crude initial bottom-up estimate of the potential ROI in solving the problem. In this form, they are a simply absolute dollar value estimates that can be compared between projects. A more sophisticated approach that allows general comparison of projects, is to apply a discount rate to future returns, so that the ROI of all potential projects is presented in terms of their net present value (NPV).[1] However, if all projects are delivering returns across the same timescale, then a comparison of estimated absolute returns will be sufficient.

The other key consideration in a prioritization exercise is the difficulty of the various options. Regardless of whether this is a prioritization between completely different problems, or subproblems of a single business issue, you will want to obtain some estimate of the relative complexity of each potential project. Some of the key considerations when making this estimate are as follows:

1. Availability. The availability of the data. If some problems relate to newer parts of the business, they will tend to have less data.
2. Quality. The quality of the data. Some source systems and business units tend to have data that is less reliable or more susceptible to noise and error.

---

[1]   C. Conlan. 2021. *The Financial Data Playbook*, Independently Published, ISBN-13: 979-8534050783

3. Size. The quantified size of the problem. Large effect sizes are generally easier to model and implement a viable solution. For example, having an impact on a churn problem that is 5 percent/yr is generally much easier than one that is 0.5 percent/yr.

4. Precursors. The presence of preexisting solutions. If you are building in a way that will extend an existing solution, then the gains are likely to be lower than attacking virgin problems. This is because your success will be judged relative to a partially solved problem.

5. Readiness. The business unit's readiness for change. This can be difficult to assess, but the first criteria is: have you met both the decision maker and someone involved in day-to-day operations? If you have and they have a shared sense of the problem and what needs to be done, then you are in a good position. If not, you need to meet these people and see how well they seem to be coordinated on the nature of the problem.

6. Simplicity. Some problems are just naturally easier to solve. You can attempt to quantify these by the number of competing hypotheses, the number of experiments you feel you need to conduct, or the number of procedural steps you can see need to be taken. It need not be perfect, but some form of quantification of project difficulty will be useful in prioritization.

Risk

As an additional factor in the prioritization process, you should ask your sponsors about the potential risk in all candidate projects. It is possible that the business sponsors have considered some elements of risk when they are proposing ROI estimates for each project, in a sense mitigating the size of the return downward according to the size and likelihood of the risks. You should, nevertheless, take the time to question them about several standard categories of data science project risk.

Project risk can take the form of difficulty with the mechanical requirements of the project; this could be access to data and systems, data quality problems, and risk involved in any third parties that supply data. Project risk can take the form of legal exposure where sensitive data is being collected or used in new systems, in ways that open the potential for loss of private data. Legal exposure, or at the very least brand damage, can also occur if the data science project produces an outcome that may be perceived as invasive or unfair. Finally, there are human risk elements related to both the team of people required to deliver the project, and the adoption of the project results by end-users. All these facets of risk should be openly discussed in the prioritization process, even if you are only working with estimates of their potential impact.

Project Plan

Once you understand these facets of each of the problems and the potential impacts of solving each of them, you are in a position to discuss project focus in a meaningful way with the client. The client will have their preferences, but businesspeople and managers will understand the language of an effort versus reward trade-off. You can simply rank all the potential projects by time/effort/difficulty and put them up against potential rewards. Be honest about lingering areas of uncertainty, put upper and lower limits on difficulty and reward if need be. This process will generally result in the client choosing the simplest problem with a nontrivial outcome.

If your client is particularly focused on solving a more difficult problem, then you need to prepare for a more drawn-out project. It is worthwhile turning the conversation toward an agreement on intermediate milestones. These milestones will help keep the project focused on delivering an outcome, rather than getting lost in minor details.

Deciding on milestones can be difficult in an endeavor like data science that is naturally driven from investigation and experimentation. The milestones should be high level, such as "initial report delivery," "second round of experimentation," and so on. The language can honor the open-ended nature of discovery, but still provide structure. In many cases, the avenues of experimentation can be mapped out in advance; doing so gives the client a sense of the scope of the work and helps them understand where time is being spent.

An agreement on milestones will also help when and if your project goes over time and budget. Having a set of intermediate results that have been delivered and are showing value builds trust and makes a budget extension conversation easier.

Summary

Focus is about knowing how to remove all the competing options and complexities and decide on a concrete project that can deliver an impact. It is fundamentally about structuring problems and prioritization. Large business problems can seem daunting if you are not able to see how they can be broken up. The goal of getting focus is to work with your client to logically separate large problems into smaller pieces, analyze and prioritize them.

You can obtain your focus in collaboration with your client using a mixture of strategies. Large problems can be broken down by searching for natural independence between component parts, or subpopulations of the effected entities. The dividing process should create a set of subproblems that can be solved independently. The final step of obtaining focus is prioritization. You work with the client to outline the effort versus reward trade-off in all potential projects, and the potential for different kinds of risk.

Ideally, you will plan the project through high-level milestones. This is particularly important on large, difficult projects. It will help you communicate the complexity of the task to your client and manage their expectations as the project progresses.

CHAPTER 9

Getting Success Metrics

The final question that needs to be answered before your project begins is: "How will we determine if the project succeeds or fails?" Ideally, if the questions asked earlier about measurement of the existing problem have been thoroughly explored, then this question will almost answer itself. You may still need to go through a process of determining the amount of change that is required in one key metric. This amount of change will take into consideration the amount that delivers sufficient value to the organization and justifies the costs of implementation.

If measurement of the problem has not been adequately explored by this juncture, then the topic of success metrics should form your line in the sand. Regardless of how nebulous the problem might seem, or how difficult it is to quantify, you should insist on hard and objective success metrics for the project. Use this requirement as a second opportunity to press for objective measures in the problem state.

Not all projects will initially have numerical metrics for success. It may be that the client is happy to have a dashboard, an MVP (Minimum Viable Product), or a system that makes a recommendation or generates a visualization. In which case the success criteria is the delivery of a tangible piece of software that provides the required output. This is in itself a metric; it is just that it only has two values: *delivered* or *not delivered*. It is not so much important what the metric is, rather that it is well defined and agreed upon by all involved.

The requirement for a specific success metric is not just about defending what you deliver. If you make the success goal as specific as possible, you are also helping the client by bringing what is important to them to the forefront of the project. It might help you determine when certain avenues are not worth pursuing or identify critical limitations from the previous lines of questioning. The success metric will also help you identify if the project is realistic. If a project appears unrealistic, it is much better to have a conversation about the feasibility of achieving a stated goal before the project begins.

Unrealistic Goals

It is not uncommon for management to set unrealistic success metrics because they feel that this might inspire you to work harder. Sometimes, however, an unrealistic goal comes from a combination of a poor understanding of what is feasible for a data science project and simple wishful thinking.

There is merit to setting ambitious goals as demonstrated by the study of Big Hairy Audacious Goals (BHAGs) that serve to inspire employees and provide an envisioned future that they can work toward.[1] However, working life will be full of feasible projects for which achieving modest goals can deliver significant and consistent value to a business. In fact, a McKinsey study determined that BHAGs that are excessively grandiose or vague can have the opposite effect of making work seem meaningless.[2]

In general, you do not want to be in a position where an audacious goal forms the criteria for success of your project. Ideally, you will want the audacious goal kept separate as a guiding principle, while your project consists of one or more intermediate steps with their own success criteria. These project goals will contribute to the vision laid out by the audacious goal, rather than deliver it in full.

I recognize that many data scientists are not able to walk away from unrealistic goals. Nevertheless, having the discussion upfront, raising your concerns and trying to mitigate the situation will still help even when the project is pushed through. You may find that stakeholders take time to absorb what you have said and are more amenable to adjustments to the project as the situation becomes clearer.

---

[1] J.C. Collins, and J.I. Porras. September/October 1996. "Building Your Company's Vision," *Harvard Business Review* 74, no. 5, pp. 65–77.

[2] T. Amabile, and S. Kramer. January 01, 2012. "How Leaders Kill Meaning at Work," McKinsey Quarterly. www.mckinsey.com/featured-insights/leadership/how-leaders-kill-meaning-at-work

If your recommendations are ignored, you should also not fall into the trap of resentment of management. There may be a range of other factors that you are unaware of. Above all else, treat these situations as a chance to experiment and look for opportunities to deliver unexpected value through insights.

Anchor to the Baseline

One way to derive strong and achievable project goals is by anchoring the project to the current baseline. The current baseline is the performance of the existing system or model. If you have clearly documented the performance of the existing process, then you can discuss project goals as incremental improvements over this performance.

To build goals in this way you will generally need to know, or have strong estimates of, the costs and benefits of a quantified change in this process. In most instances, this will have come from your discussion of the problem context with the client. For example, you will know what each instance of fraud, or customer churn, or late delivery costs the organization on average. You will also know what an intervention costs them, both when it is done correctly or mistakenly.

Detailed knowledge about these costs and benefits allows you to estimate the performance requirements of a model in advance of building it.[3] As a part of research in this area, we have produced an open-source python library to help with this process that the reader should feel free to explore and extend as necessary.[4]

The absence of a concrete understanding of the costs and benefits associated with individual outcomes should be treated as a red flag. If you have not drilled into this level of detail, then you should attempt this before moving forward with the project. The general exception to this rule

---

[3] J. Hawkins. December 18–19, 2020. "Minimum Viable Model Estimates for Machine Learning Projects," *Proceedings of the 6th International Conference on Computer Science, Engineering and Applications (CSEA 2020)* 10, no. 18. pp. 37–46,

[4] J. Hawkins. August 2021. "MinViME/Minimum Viable Model Estimator," *Software Impacts* 9. https://doi.org/10.1016/j.simpa.2021.100073

are projects concerning new business processes or products for which the information does not yet exist. Even in these instances it is worthwhile collecting estimates of these values, which should be your fallback option when dealing with clients that are reluctant to provide this level of detail.

If the detailed cost and benefit information is unobtainable in detail, or as an estimate, then you can steer the conversation toward estimates of impact under incremental improvements. This is a gentle way of probing for similar information, but in aggregate. For example, rather than knowing that the average cost of a fraud is 10,000 dollars, you learn that a 1 percent improvement in fraud prediction would reduce fraud costs by approximately one million dollars. These numbers are in principle derivable from each other, but doing so requires knowledge of not only the base rates and volumes but also an understanding of intervention costs as well as the implementation and operational costs of new systems inside the organization. The reason this aggregate approach can be effective is that it operates at the level of understanding typically undertaken by business sponsors. They will usually have extensive experience in writing business cases for projects that juggle a wide range of high-level costs and derive their quantitative strength from statistics derived from other projects in the organization. To engage your client in this level of discussion involves requesting something like the following:

"What is the approximate business impact of improving the identification of fraud cases by five percent?"

"What is the impact of falsely identifying an additional one percent of transactions as fraud cases?"

The goal with this line of questioning is to get the client to discuss estimates of incremental business value and costs. You should probe for insight under different levels of incremental change and question them about any potential source of financial impact. Taking the high-level impact approach will sometimes result in the client realizing that they need to understand the fine details of the process. The successive rounds of questioning and answering can help them see that small details can matter in aggregate. In other words, the high-level discussion, in terms the sponsor is used to, encourages them to think through what it means to implement a data science solution. In doing so, they can realize why data science projects typically require much more granular details.

Summary

The final check point before beginning the execution phase of your project is to obtain concrete success metrics. Regardless of everything that has come prior to this point, you should not advance without concrete success criteria. For many projects these criteria may be the delivery of a report that outlines a series of experimental results, or a data visualization. The metric need not be anchored to specific business value, but if the client does expect measurable business impact, then you should be especially vigilant. Thoroughly explore the expected impact of incremental changes to the process and ensure that improvements are both achievable and that the estimated impact is realistic.

PART II

Execution

CHAPTER 10

Getting Data Updates

By this stage of the project, you will have a very clear idea of what the problem is and what some of the potential solutions might look like. You should also have seen some form of data that illustrates the nature of the problem. As discussed in the chapters on context and measurement, you will have potentially been through iterations on the initial data to iron out any issues with how it is extracted and the fields it contains.

As the project shifts to the delivery phase, you will need to have an agreement with the client about the data that will be used for the analysis and experimentation. This may involve extracting a larger historical set of data or obtaining extracts from all source systems that could contribute to the solution. In the process of obtaining the working data set, it is worthwhile coming to some agreement with the client about how data will be structured. This structure should apply to the initial data extraction, and to any updates that are delivered as the project progresses.

Problem and Data Alignment

In the sections on problem context, we discussed the importance of seeing data that is coherent with the problem that has been described to you. That data should have demonstrated the volumes of problem cases and some of the key characteristics. It should have indicated something about the nature of the systems that collect that data, and it would have given you an opportunity to start looking for biases and issues with the data.

When you start working on the project execution you require a data set in which these issues have been removed. Far too much of a project execution can be eaten up by unnecessary iterations on data quality. There are a range of standard problems that occur when clients prepare data for you. So common in fact that you are generally better off anticipating them and communicating upfront about what you need in the data.

Clean and Representative Signal

The most critical requirement is that the data contains a measurement of the problem state that is both coherent with the problem statement and is illustrative of the entire scope of the problem. For example, it may be the set of all customers from the last five years with a flag indicating those who have churned over that period. It could alternatively be all the sales leads pursued over the last year with a flag indicating success or failure. The critical thing is that whatever the signal variables are, they are defined in the same way that has been discussed with the project sponsors, and the pattern you observe is the same as the problem that was described to you.

It is generally better to obtain all records over an extended period, even when a random sample might be sufficient. You do not want to complicate your life with trying to diagnose issues with someone else's random sampling process. Having a data set of the entire population allows you to control the sampling process and provides ample opportunity for multiple rounds of testing. Obtaining records across a wide span of time is also desirable because to allows you to put aside a slice of the most recent data that can be used as an out-of-time test set. Out-of-time testing can, on occasion, reveal that a problem has a dependence on time itself.

You may need to go through multiple iterations to get to this stage. Sometimes organization will only provide data about one half of the problem. For example, they may only provide the records of the customers who churned in the period. You may encounter some resistance when asking for the entire customer base. A manager might respond with comment like:

> Why do you need to see the customers who didn't churn? It is the churning customers we want you to focus on.

These conversations can be difficult and frustrating to navigate, particularly if the project is meant to have started and you are asking for more data. It is far better to have the conversation with the client upfront, explaining that you need to see records for all customers to understand what differentiates the problem cases. You want to see multiple snapshots of data over time, to understand how systems and processes might have

GETTING DATA UPDATES   91

changed. Most importantly, you need the signal or measurement to be calculated in the same way, with the same source data, over the entire period for all customers, because this is the only way to isolate potential influences and interventions.

You need to develop your own analogies and methods of describing why these issues are important. Here is an example I sometimes use when making this point to a client: Please think back to when you were learning mathematics in school. It was just as important to know when you got an answer correct as when you got it wrong. The same principle applies to applying data science methods to analyze customer data. We need to see examples of when customers are happy, just as much as we need to see unhappy customers.

Once you have data that represents the entire population, you need to again verify that the nature of the problem is maintaining its coherence with the data. We indicated in an earlier chapter that this would be an iterative process. Every time your work leads you to request new data, you need to run basic coherence checks. These need not be arduous, simple checks of the number of problem cases, or records with values above a given threshold, or proportions of records in key groups. Automating these tests with a script is ideal, which justifies another key topic we will discuss at the end of this chapter: subsequent data updates should always conform to the same structure.

Proxy Signals

The only acceptable circumstances in which you can move forward with no direct data describing the problem is when there is no existing direct measurement of the problem, or the process has started so recently that there has not been time to collect sufficient data. In these circumstances, the only viable approach will be to develop synthetic proxy signal from which to work.

Aside from the many technical problems with developing an acceptable proxy signal, there are multiple project management issues. First, you need the presence of mind to maintain awareness that you are always working with a proxy, and any conclusions need to be filtered through that awareness.

You then need to ensure that the stakeholders understand any potential limitations of the proxy. Most proxy signals will tend to under- or overestimate a problem, depending on how they are constructed. Often it can be better to use the language of boundary constraints when using proxy signals of some kind. For example, late payments are commonly used in consumer finance as a proxy of potential loan defaults. One of the useful aspects of this proxy signal is that it places a short-term upper bound of what it is a proxy for; you cannot default on a loan without first missing a payment.

Update Protocols

It is not uncommon that you will require multiple copies of the data set as the project progresses. Perhaps, as the project drags on, you will want to request an update to check how the most recent data looks. Perhaps, you will discover that they have additional data fields that would be desirable to add to the data set.

It is worthwhile putting in place an agreement on what the format of this data is when it is provided to you. This need not be particularly onerous. A list of column names and data types that will appear in a CSV (Comma Separated Values), or Excel, file is a minimal starting point.

I have been caught out by not having such an agreement in place multiple times. I received an updated data set (from the same data source) with different numbers of columns in different orders, with different names, simply because the technician extracting it was re-creating the scripts every time. It is possible to manipulate and rearrange the data, but that work is tedious and takes you out of the frame of mind of solving the actual problem. Solving unnecessary and avoidable problems impedes your efficiency as a data scientist. Having a common format for data updates, means that you can have generic scripts to check for errors, to rerun analysis and evaluate models. It means greater code reuse and with it less chance of errors.

Summary

There is a nonnegotiable requirement for you to have a data set that accurately reflects the problem as it was described to you. The combination of a human description of the problem and empirical measurements that agree with them provides a solid foundation from which to begin your project. You should anticipate problems with how the data will be provided, by having a clear and detailed discussion in advance of the data being extracted. Ideally, this will involve a specification of the structure of the data so that later updates can be used without needing to process them or change your code.

CHAPTER 11

Data Familiarity

Data exploration and visualization is a field that straddles the topics of both understanding data as well as using it for communication. The process of understanding data contributes to multiple stages of a data science project. There are many books and articles that cover the specific techniques that are used to understand variables in a data set. Some articles will focus predominantly on visual techniques,[1] while others emphasize statistical and algorithmic methods.[2] Rather than review the specifics of these techniques, the focus on this chapter will be on how and why they are used, as well as aspects of the data exploration process that are underemphasized and affect project delivery.

Checking for Errors

It is a mistake to assume that the data you have been provided has been extracted in an error-free process. Performing analysis on faulty data will undermine your project and endanger delivery. You need to validate that the data you have been given is what the client thinks it is.

Typically, your sponsor will have asked a junior analyst or database admin to extract a data set for you. If you take the data you are given at face value, then you are assuming all of the following:

1. The sponsor clearly communicated what was required in the data set.
2. The junior understood what they were asking.
3. The junior was able to translate that into an extraction script without error.

[1] P. Dave. 2020. "15 Data Exploration Techniques to Go From Data to Insights," *Blog Post*. https://towardsdatascience.com/15-data-exploration-techniques-to-go-from-data-to-insights-93f66e6805df

[2] M. Liu, Z. Wang, Z. Gong, J. Yoon, and X. Wang. 2020, "Data Exploration," *ML@CMU Blog Post*. https://blog.ml.cmu.edu/2020/08/31/2-data-exploration/

All these assumptions are regularly incorrect. To make matters more complicated it is also possible that politics is involved. For example, the sponsor might be asking for something that does not exist, but the junior does not feel empowered enough to tell them. So, instead of speaking up the junior generates a data set that approximates as closely as they can what has been asked for.

A simple way to determine whether the data is what the sponsor thinks it is, is by feeding back to them some core statistics and plots from the data. For example, if the data was all sales leads over the last 12 months, give them the total number of customers, the total number of sales, and the total number of unsuccessful leads. Perhaps then give them a bar chart showing the monthly breakdown, or the break down across dates or regions. The sponsor will generally have a good macroscopic view of the business and should quickly identify if the data you have is an accurate reflection of what they were expecting to see. If your client is comfortable with all the numbers and charts you give them, then you can have some confidence that there were not major errors in the data extraction scripts.

Eyeballing

In the process of verifying with the client that the data is correct, you will have started down the path of getting familiar with the data. The process of eyeballing a variety of histograms and scatter plots is an invaluable step in the data analysis path. There are several features of the data you are looking for that will influence your process moving forward. The two key areas are the omissions or biases present in the data, and the balance between relationships and randomness.

Omissions and Biases

Plotting histograms of various parameters, and the number of records across time will help you identify if there are missing records in the data. These may arise because of errors in the extraction script, they might be due to historical problems with logging systems and data capture. Or they may be due to inherent biases in the data; for example, it might be that some salespeople do not have any unsuccessful leads because they don't enter their leads into the Customer Relationship Management (CRM) system until they are sure that it will convert (as I described earlier, this exact scenario has happened to me).

In all these cases, knowing about omissions and biases will help you determine how to treat the data in a final analysis. Do you need to exclude some data, reweight certain data points, or generate some deliberate features designed to minimize the biases? There are many things that can be done to mitigate these issues, but only if you know they exist. Hence the criticality of the data familiarity stage.

Relationships and Randomness

Eyeballing is not only about uncovering omissions and biases. Some very simple visualizations can help you understand the key relationships in the data between the target variables and other business metrics or features. As I imagine most readers are aware, scatter plots allow you to look at pairwise relationships between each of your variables. For example, in Figure 11.1 we see several scatter plots that quickly demonstrate some of the main kinds of relationships you might find between variables.

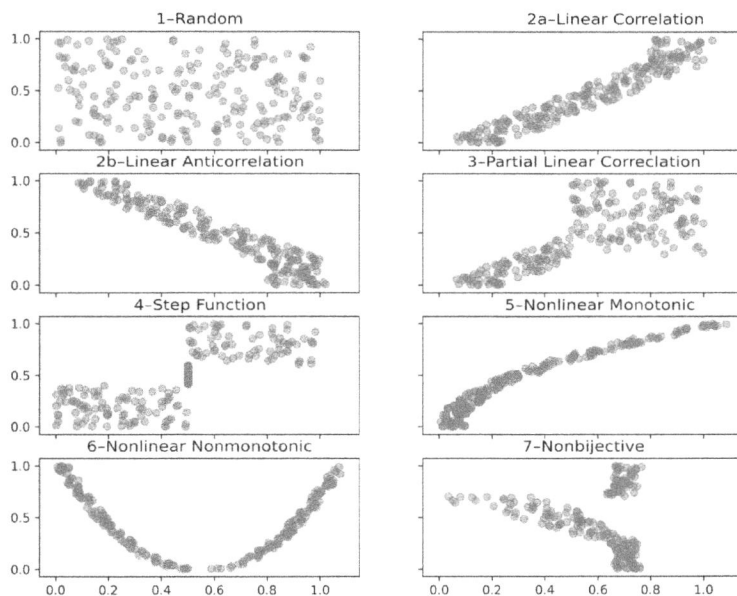

Figure 11.1 Unitary data relationships

1. No discernible relationship
2. Linear correlations
3. Partial linear correlation
4. Step functions
5. Nonlinear monotonic relationships
6. Nonlinear nonmonotonic relationships
7. Nonbijective relationships

The last of these relationships is distinguished by whether you can expect there to be more than one grouping of potential y values for a given x value. The nonbijective category permits any kind of shape that is not entirely random. It constitutes a relationship that cannot be captured by a true mathematical function. As such, its presence often indicates the existence of additional mitigating variables. In other words, it is one indication of a nonunivariate relationship.

Each of these specific types of plots is an illustrative and informative depiction of potential relationships. In real data you will very rarely see clean relationships. Most business problems consist of data with weak and noisy relationships between variables. In this regard, your real-world projects will be very different from tutorials and academic exercises. The scatter plots you generate will most likely be fuzzy balls of points with vague elongation where some correlation exists.

In most data science projects these visualizations will be more useful in identifying redundant variables, or mistakes. Clean textbook correlations are more likely to occur when you have been given a data set in which there are duplicates of some columns, or there are variables that share some source data for derivation. By plotting all variables against each other, your eye will be drawn to those that are closely related and allow you to identify these redundant variables.

You should be wary of instances in which you do see clean relationships between your feature variables and the target or business metric variables. In most cases, this will be because your target variable has been derived from these other variables. The primary exception to this rule will be for data derived from a self-contained mechanistic process; for example, the inputs, machine telemetry, and outputs of an industrial process could easily contain very clean deterministic processes.

Explainability

An additional dimension to the process of becoming familiar with the data is determining how you will use it for communication. Even if your visualizations of univariate relationships reveal very weak patterns, they can be an indispensable tool for explaining your results. Human beings respond strongly to explanations that use visual aids and answer various kinds of why questions.[3] In data science work, examples might include: why does this problem occur? why does your model work? or why do we expect that this change will have an impact? A visual presentation of relationships can aid in explaining any one of these questions.

Understanding a complex pattern in the data can be rendered far more intelligible when presented as a sequence of individual relationships. A logical place to start is with the strongest observed relationship, and then adding layers of additional contributing factors. If your client has emphasized some of their hypotheses about what drives a problem, then those are a natural set of variables to include in any explanation. If the relationships are real, it is likely that they are visible as step functions or very near linear. It is not often that humans are able to instinctively detect complex nonlinear relationships in business data. If your client has ideas about the causal relationships without having done data analysis, then discussing those hypotheses with the aid of some simple visualizations can be useful in progressing the client's understanding, and your relationship along with it.

Relationships between multiple variables can be, and usually are, much more complicated. The extent to which you want to delve deeper into visualization depends on what you are trying to achieve, how much data you have, and how much the client wants the problem explained versus solved. If the client has proposed several strong hypotheses about the drivers of a problem, then a technique like a two-way partial dependence plot will allow you to illustrate potential interactions between these factors.[4]

---

[3] L. LeFever. June 2018, 2013. *Battle-Tested Tips for Effective Explanations.* (Harvard Business Review).

[4] J.H. Friedman. 2001. "Greedy Function Approximation: A Gradient Boosting Machine," *The Annals of Statistics* 29, no. 5, pp. 1189–1232.

Summary

Exploring your data visually is a great way to determine whether the business problem is as it has been described. You can also determine if there are any potential issues with the data collection and preparation processes. Finally, univariate plots allow you to determine the relationships between variables, identify problems, and build a productive dialogue with your stakeholders about the nature of the problem and how it might be solved.

CHAPTER 12

Data Science Methods

The bulk of the execution phase of the project resides with data manip-ulation, model building, and the design of algorithms to solve the core problems posed in the project. There are a wide variety of directions a data science project can go at this juncture. So many directions, that it is difficult to provide general guidelines on why they succeed or fail. In this chapter, we will briefly outline the most common kinds of data science projects and some characteristics that influence their respective success. These project types are insights and analytics, pattern discovery, predictive modeling, recommendation systems, and optimization. You should note that this is neither exhaustive nor generated from the same level of a tech-nical hierarchy. These topics are chosen simply because they are the most common general themes for data science projects from the perspective of what the business is trying to achieve.

Insights and Analytics

An insights project is generally defined by a client who is pushing for an understanding of their problem, without prioritizing a material solution. It may be as simple as arranging multiple data sets into visually consum-able format or helping them define composite metrics that summarize the status quo of key areas of the business. Many data scientists denounce these projects as being outside the domain of real data science. Regardless of what you believe, they form a significant part of the landscape of proj-ects that are currently given to data scientists. As such, it would be remiss not to cover them here.

If you are a data scientist who is being asked to help a client under-stand a business problem, without being given specific prediction targets or business metrics to influence, then the project likely resides in the domain of insights. The key rule of thumb for these projects is that you should strive to ensure that what you present can be tied back to the business in an actionable way. You may not have been given business outcomes as an objective, but they will be part of the filter through which your work is consumed and judged. So, as you build, plot, or design these projects, take care to continually ask yourself "how could someone act on this information?" I will dedicate the next chapter to discussing these projects in more detail.

Pattern Discovery

A pattern discovery project has some overlap with an insights project, in the sense that neither are geared toward a specific material impact on a business process. In pattern discovery, you will be provided with data with which the client expects you to discover patterns that can be used to solve business problems or unlock new streams of revenue. Sometimes, the instructions can be as vague as find some value in this data or look for some exploitable patterns.

If you have followed the rest of this book, you will have been doing your best to get a more concrete goal. If this goal remains absent, then you will be stuck with a pattern discovery project. There is a certain freedom in these projects, particularly when you understand the business domain well. They are an opportunity for you to deliver something novel and impactful. That opportunity also comes with a great deal of risk; finding novel and substantial ways to monetize data is a difficult job and success is a rare outcome.

A good way to mitigate that risk is to look for ways that the data can be used to augment or improve existing parts of the business. In other words, do not restrict your thoughts to just blue-sky novel business applications. The better you know the existing business model and processes, the easier it will be to identify immediate applications of data. We will discuss approaches to pattern discovery in one of the following chapters.

Predictive Modeling

Predictive modeling projects should need the least explanation for most data scientists. You should have been given a business problem that involves knowing something in advance of it happening, and you should have a data set containing this quantity as a well-defined target variable. Ideally, you will have a strong understanding of how the prediction can be used for the benefit of the business process.

For example, consider a business that wants to improve the click through rate of their offers by matching offers to customers. They will give you a data set containing all offers presented to their user base, and the details about which were successful. The model will be used to choose which offer to present whenever an eligible customer appears on their website. There are many, many variations of this setup, but the logic of thinking through and managing the project remains very similar.

One of the most overlooked steps in predictive modeling projects is to create solid baselines. This means evaluating simple models, but also evaluating nonmodels as well. What is the simplest nonmachine learning approach you could take? It should be informed by what you know about the domain, the business process, and the class of model you are building. For example, the mean response regressor as a baseline for a regression model, or the majority class for classifier. If your deep neural network does not outperform a model that outputs the mean of the distribution, then it is not adding value. We will dedicate many sections to discussing common pitfalls and strategies for effective predictive modeling in the subsequent chapters.

Recommendation Systems

In some instances, you are asked to build systems that make predictions, but you are given weak, or insufficient, historical data. One class of these problems will be instances where you have some examples of behavior, but not canonical examples of ideal behavior. As such you will not have target variables for supervised learning. In some of these cases you will be looking at building recommender systems.

The boundary between ideal applications of multiclass prediction versus recommender systems is determined by the nature of the process. Recommendation systems become appropriate with large numbers of products, from a catalog that changes regularly and low tendency for repeat purchase. All these qualities combine to make multiclass supervised learning less feasible and effective. True applications of recommendation systems are rarer than is generally thought, not all companies are Netflix or Amazon. In the vast majority of business cases, recommendation system style results can be better achieved with multiclass, or next best offer, models.

Just as with predictive modeling, the most common mistake is inadequate baselining. In the case of recommendation systems, the naïve baseline can be something as simple as just returning the most popular product. In addition, it is worthwhile evaluating simple machine learning solutions as well to justify the specific recommendation algorithm you are looking to implement.

Optimization

On the surface, the meaning of the term optimization is clear. In everyday language, it simply means adjusting a process that results in an improved outcome. The existence of the common language definition adds complication to managing optimization projects. Businesspeople have expectations about what it would mean. Technical people will expect that the optimization is subject to certain limitations, and people from an Operations Research background will have specific technical expectations about what is needed to even start down the process of optimization.

It is worthwhile getting in front of these issues through open dialogue. As soon as it is clear that there is a sense in which the project will involve process optimization, have a discussion with all involved about what they mean by that term. Identify exactly what is being optimized and what everyone's expectations are. Real-world projects that fit perfectly into the confines of optimization according to the structures of academic research are less common than other notions of optimization. More common is to have a process that is well understood but loosely quantified. It will produce business outcomes that are partly monitored and measured. The constraints and action space will be loosely understood and require significant investigation.

In some instances, optimization projects depend on stochastic processes that need to be modeled before they can be optimized. This situation brings with it a suite of challenges around the representative nature of the data and the extent to which causal relationships can be captured. In many instances, these projects will require experimentation within the real-world process. This means you will need to convince the business to allow you to vary the free parameters in a way that allows you to observe the impacts on the business process.

Experimentation like this may result in a solution in and of itself. Alternatively, it will give you an improved data set for building models that can capture the causal structure of the process. However, experimentation is costly for businesses, not just the costs of the project, but because the process of random sampling will usually result in some wastage, lost sales, and so on. As soon as your project is heading toward optimization, you need to determine the amount of experimentation that needs to be done and start getting the approval. Make sure the stakeholders understand how and why this needs to be done.

Summary

There are a wide variety of types of data science projects in a technical delivery sense. Each of these project types have their own requirements and their own pitfalls. In this chapter, we have extracted three key themes across them all. First, you should always strive to make your work actionable. Regardless of how open-ended the research seems, you should prioritize approaches that can be tied back to the business. Secondly, you should ensure that you build baseline models, ideally multiple of them, each designed to test (and rule out) hypotheses about alternative approaches. Finally, you should aim to determine what resources you will need early in the project. Optimization projects typically require some experimentation that comes with its own costs to the business. Once you know the kind of data science project you have, you should start communicating with stakeholders about what it will require.

CHAPTER 13

Insights and Analytics

Insights and Analytics projects are not always given to data scientists. Many organizations have dedicated analytics teams; however those teams can be tied up with generating standard reports, so bespoke analytics requests can spill over to the data science team. Analytics is also common in the data science work of organizations that are early in the path of data science adoption. Analytics work can also be given to junior data scientists to help them develop data preparation skills and to familiarize them with the business. The key to executing these projects well lies in developing the right data assets and metrics, in order to answer the business questions being asked of you.

Data Acquisition

To deliver many kinds of data science projects you require multiple sources integrated into a cohesive whole. For insights and analytics projects, this is potentially more difficult because of the maturity of the organization or business process. You will need to pay particular attention to determine where all the data will come from. Is it already prepared for you inside a Group Data Warehouse (GDW)? Or do you need to go chasing it from different parts of the organization? If it is the latter, then you will likely find it residing in multiple source systems, in different formats and perhaps varying levels of granularity. There can be a significant engineering effort in just getting all the required data streams together and joining them into a coherent whole.

You can increase the probability of your project succeeding by quickly understanding the difficulty of accessing and integrating all these data sources. You will want the project decision makers to be aware of the marginal costs of including each information source, as well as the potential value of those data sources. It is easy to burn project budget trying to integrate every data source that was mentioned by your stakeholders.

Generally, they will care more about getting a result, than including all possible data. Helping your stakeholders make these rationalizations about the data to include is part of the data science job.

Metrics

We have spent several chapters already talking about metrics of various kinds. For an insights and analytics project, you will typically be focused only on aggregate business level metrics, those that relate to the kinds of strategic decisions made by management. These metrics will generally be some mixture of direct revenue-related metrics (sales, accounts, activity, etc.), cost-related metrics (raw materials, infrastructure, energy, labor, etc.), and a range of metrics that indicate intangible business fundamentals that have long-term effects (customer satisfaction, brand recall, equality, etc.).

In many instances, you will find yourself being asked to monitor a range of internal signals that are proxy metrics indirectly related to one or more of these core aspects. The reason for these proxy metrics is often that your project is sponsored by a single line of business that is not directly responsible for the sources of revenue or costs. Instead, they manage some aspect of the business that indirectly affects these business outcomes.

In an ideal world these metrics would all be predefined and centrally stored for transparent use across a business. In reality, there are often barriers of access to data sources inside many organizations. You will likely need to work with your stakeholders on the definition of the metrics and uncover the complexities in deriving them from the available data.

Dimensions

The metrics that an organization wants to monitor will be rendered intelligible by a range of other variables that determine the important subgroups or categories to drill into. In reporting and visualization these are often called the available reporting dimensions. Common dimensions are product type, customer type, business division, region, or date. The idea is to provide sufficient diversity in the ways that a business user can separate the data into groups, or add dimensions to a plot, that they can answer common business questions. There are three competing tensions in the generation of dimensions:

1. What the business can act on.
2. What is computationally feasible.
3. What is compliant with privacy and security.

Maintaining a very large number of dimensions has become feasible in the era of big data and cloud computing. But it can still incur significant costs. The cloud computing providers make it trivial to run large-scale inefficient queries on your data. It is only later that you learn the cost of that inefficiency.

There is another cost to high-dimensional data analytics: multiple hypothesis testing. When the number of dimensions is very high, then it becomes probable that patterns can be found that are the result of random variation. This is equivalent to the phenomenon of drawing false conclusions through multiple hypothesis testing.[1] The core idea being that if you look at enough combinations of enough data then you will find something striking. Contrary to popular opinion in data and analytics, if you are involved in the design and build of self-service analytical tools, then you would better serve the business by restricting the number of dimensions to a smaller set of actionable and high-value variables.

Visualizations

While tabular data is acceptable to some organizations and stakeholders, it is generally faster to absorb insights via visualization of data. Bar charts utilize our innate ability to perceive proportional differences in quantities. Consumers of bar charts typically do not need training to interpret the data, as long as the construction of chart is done in such a way as to utilize our natural perceptions. However, there are subtleties to the way people

---

[1] S.Y. Chen, Z. Feng, and X. Yi. 2017. "A General Introduction to Adjustment for Multiple Comparisons," *Journal of Thoracic Disease* 9, no. 6, pp. 1725–1729. https://doi.org/10.21037/jtd.2017.05.34

interpret the natural groupings and explain what a visualization means based on the type of chart that is used.[2]

The key to effective visualization is then the art of designing the visualization such that it works with our visual system and psychological predispositions. The art of good information visualization is detailed and sophisticated. Contrary to popular opinion it is not synonymous with being a good visual designer. Many infographics that are shared on social networks are guilty of fundamental design flaws. These can be understood as either stemming from naivete, or a desire to make the data say something specific. There are multiple excellent books that describe the fundamental ways that visualizations can be used to deceive. "A field guide to lies and statistics" by Daniel Levitin,[3] or the now classic book "How to lie with statistics" by Darrell Huff,[4] are both concise and entertaining introductions to this topic.

In order to do data visualization very well requires specific study. The work of Edward R. Tufte, in particular his book "The Visual Display of Qualitative Data,"[5] is highly recommended for the reader who wants to produce exceptional work. This work is partly a history of graphical representation of data, and partly the culmination of his research into the theory and practice of using graphical representation of data to enhance reasoning.

Although the field of data visualization is dense and detailed, there are a few simple principles that will allow you to create visualizations that are truthful and informative. If in doubt you should use standard charts like bar charts or scatter plots. You should avoid artistic flourishes that distort proportions between data, like three dimensional effects. You should always show the units on axes, show the complete axis starting from zero and do not cherry pick what you do and do not show in the plots.[6]

---

[2] D. Peebles, and A. Nadia. 2015. "Expert Interpretation of Bar and Line Graphs: The Role of Graphicacy in Reducing the Effect of Graph Format," *Frontiers in Psychology* 6. https://doi.org/10.3389/fpsyg.2015.01673

[3] D. Levitin. 2018. *A field guide to lies and statistics*. Penguin Books.

[4] D. Huff. 1954. *How to Lie with Statistics* (New York, NY: Norton).

[5] E.R. Tufte. 2001. *The Visual Display of Quantitative Information*, Second Edition. Graphics Press.

[6] E. Murray. April 04, 2019. "Why Do Bar Charts Work?" Forbes Magazine. www.forbes.com/sites/evamurray/2019/04/04/why-do-bar-charts-work

Data Gluttony

In earlier chapters, we explored the process of asking questions to define a project. For an insights and analytics project, the line of questioning should have detected that the key problem was an absence of insight into how certain aspects of the business were changing over time. It could be that management does not have easy access to the information, or the access comes too late to be actionable. The answers should have all pointed toward an inability by management to simply know what they need to, when they need to, in order to make effective decisions.

Once these factors become clear you should make an attempt to start ranking the requested metrics in order of importance. After being starved of information, management can fall straight into data gluttony and ask for a great many different metrics. If you indulge them, then the project can result in a complicated dashboard that provides little assistance because the data is simply overwhelming.

Over time, data gluttony can result in a multitude of reports that are sent out and never read. A head of analytics once described to me his experience of taking over a division and discovering large numbers of cumbersome and unmaintainable reporting processes. Failing to find any method of understanding who used which report for what purpose, he just started turning them off. If no one complained within three months he concluded the report was redundant and it was archived. His simple approach resulted in a significant simplification of the entire process.

Perhaps the meaning of data gluttony is self-evident. But in case it is not, the idea is that when people are greedy about the data they want to visualize, it can be counterproductive. Much in the same way that over-eating is poor for your health, consumption of excessive amounts of data can result in the paralysis of inaction. In order to avoid data gluttony, and bring focus to the project, you need to ask questions designed to uncover the relative importance of all metrics that are being requested. The two most important dimensions are asking what decisions will be made based on those metrics, and how regularly those decisions will be made. You should quickly find that some metrics will not be relevant to any decisions whatsoever. If you find that all metrics are related to one or more decisions, then press for details about how they are used in the decision. For example,

What value would this metric need to take before you decide to
do XYZ?

Or

Can you give me an example of the options that might be considered in such a decision? How would this metric let you choose
between them?

You are looking for a polite way to identify metrics that are not actually going to be used in the decision-making process. Management can
sometimes ask for metrics because they are not sure at the outset what is
going to be useful in decision making. They may believe that until they
see the data they will not know what will be useful. This approach is usually misguided, through rigorous thought and examination many metrics
can be ruled out. It may seem harmless to provide metrics that add little
value, were it not for the fact that these low-impact metrics are competing
for screen real estate and mental space with all the metrics that do matter.

After you engage in a detailed evaluation process, you should have
annotations on all the requested metrics. You should know whether they
have an impact on a real decision, and you should know how regularly
that decision needs to be made. These annotations can then drive the
design of the project solution.

Building Dashboards and Reports

The final deliverable for insights and analytics projects is the data presented in a consumable form. Whatever form that is, you will be aiming
to structure it such that the presentation directly supports the business
decisions. In an ideal world you would have a small number of metrics
that support one or two key decisions. This makes the process of building
the deliverable very straightforward. If instead, you find yourself dealing
with some of the other issues raised in this chapter, then you will need to
build something that walks the line between solving the problem versus
delivering what is being asked for. Both of those criteria will be used to

determine the success of the project and you need to attempt to fulfill both constraints even though they may be in conflict. I suggest the following general strategy to attempt to satisfy the tension between these criteria.

1. Start by building your report or dashboard so that each concrete decision has a dedicated panel or screen that contains only those metrics you are convinced are used for that decision.
2. For any metrics that are only relevant once they reach a given level, make them optional inclusions, or make them apparent via an alert system.
3. Add an additional panel or screen, perhaps called something like General, Overview, or Summary, and add all the additional metrics that were not connected to any of the actual decisions, but have been insisted upon by the clients.

Your client may want to move some of the noninfluential metrics onto the decision-making panels. Although you can make the case for effective decision support by only showing what is needed, ultimately you need to be prepared to make concessions. You should always be aware that even when your questioning did not reveal a relationship between a specific metric and the decision making, that does not mean one does not exist. We all engage in decision-making processes that we are not able to articulate. The fact that your stakeholder does not have the awareness of how the information is used, does not mean that they are not using it at all.

After applying this process, you should have a business insights tool that actively supports decision making and delivers what had been requested. It will strike a balance between solving the real problem and satisfying the customer's demands. The ultimate test will be whether you are able to improve the efficiency or effectiveness of their decision making.

Summary

The overarching principle of achieving business impact with insights and analytics is to support decision making through presentation of data.

The data will need to be accurate and timely, but it will also benefit from simplicity and restraint. In many instances, your core job as an insights data scientist is to help your stakeholders identify the exact data they need to make better decisions. The reader is referred to the book *Introduction to Business Analytics*[7] for an overview of analytics terminology and techniques, including practical exercises using both Microsoft Excel and Tableau.

---

[7] M. Navbavi, D.L. Olson, and W.S. Boyce. 2021. *Introduction to Business Analytics*, Second Edition (New York, NY: Business Expert Press).

CHAPTER 14

Pattern Discovery

The criteria that separate a pattern discovery project from an insights and analytics project can be quite subtle. The language of pattern discovery is sometimes used by stakeholders who really want you to create visualizations so they can identify the patterns themselves. The key distinction you need to make is the extent to which they are prepared for patterns to be discovered algorithmically. As an extension to this, you need to determine what would constitute proof to them that a pattern is genuine. Does it need to be something that can be explicitly visualized? Or would they be satisfied with quantitative criteria that the pattern exists?

In general, a pattern discovery project will be less prescriptive than other kinds of projects. This brings with it great uncertainty and potential for failure. However, there are a range of ways that you can impose structure on a pattern discovery project, giving it a more pragmatic focus than it might otherwise possess. Note that while many of the techniques used for pattern discovery would fall into the family of unsupervised learning techniques, I deliberately use the term pattern discovery because there are others that do not.

Finding Structure

There are two common situations in which pattern discovery projects emerge. The first is when the client has a data asset they want to monetize, the second is when they have a suspected business problem, but no strong ideas about what the driving forces are. In both situations, there is potential to anchor the project to more concrete constraints.

In the case of a suspected business problem, the approach outlined in the initial chapters will have guided you through a sufficient information-gathering process. The problem may still be ambiguous and require pattern discovery techniques, but you will also have a strong understanding of the business to guide you.

In the case of data monetization projects, you will want to find structure in the form of business models that the organization is strategically open to. Are they interested in selling data? Are they interested in selling reports to other related businesses? Or are they interested in finding patterns that can be used to enhance their existing business models?

All the above questions can be asked in the framing stage of the project. They will help you conceive of and prioritize experiments. They will also, as we discuss later, help you interface with some of the design choices when working with algorithms.

A Common Use Case

There is one general application domain that contains examples of projects that routinely need a pattern discovery approach. This is the domain of security and fraud detection. Systems administrators have good reason to be paranoid that there might be unwanted activity going on inside their networks. They might explicitly ask for an algorithmic exploration of network traffic or server usage that might highlight potential nefarious activity.

The same will be true of projects for government agencies that investigate tax evasion or insider trading, as well as banks looking for fraudulent transactions. This situation applies to any domain in which you are searching for illicit activity wherein the patterns of behavior will change over time. In fact, the actors involved are incentivized to change and mask their behaviors, as that is what allows them to continue as successful criminals.

In most of these situations there will be labeled data sets of known historical cases, but you will expect that there are other cases of illicit activity that go unnoticed. These common factors mean that a common solution pattern is routinely applied across all these use cases:

1. Use a predictive model on historical cases to identify repetitions of past infringements.
2. Use a pattern discovery algorithm (often anomaly detection) to discover potential new instances.
3. Combine both into an intervention pathway that is partly automated, and partly human moderated.

In many instances the specific pattern discovery algorithm will change, it may even be bespoke, but the overall structure remains. The power of this solution is it acknowledges that we can deal with known and unknown patterns of activity in different ways, and yet combine them into a system that permits concrete actions and interventions.

Mixed Projects

It is not uncommon for a project to include some pattern discovery along with other approaches. As outlined in the previous section, pattern discovery can support predictive modeling to identify previously unobserved events. Pattern discovery can also be used in conjunction with insights and analytics, wherein patterns are surfaced as visualizations.

When these mixture projects occur, they provide an opportunity for additional structure. For example, in the fraud scenario discussed in the previous section, the target of pattern discovery is not entirely unknown— it is new patterns of fraud. The sponsor is not looking for you to find interesting ways that genuine customers are using their credit cards, they want to solve fraud problems. In other words, the type of patterns they want discovered are constrained.

Similar constraint occurs when pattern discovery is mixed with other techniques, or in other domains. For example, if you are doing insights and analytics work on customer churn, your client will likely be asking to visualize key dimensions they expect to be related to churn. They may not know what it is that drives the churn problem, but they have suspicions. Their suspicions will determine the combinations of data they want visualized.

The client might be asking for pattern discovery on data sets they have no intuitions about. For example, what do the application logs for usage of apps and websites reveal about the patterns of customer churn. In this instance, your pattern discovery is constrained by a specific target—what can you find that correlates with churn.

Some pattern discovery techniques are constrained to only work for certain applications. Association Rule mining, for example, by the nature of the algorithm helps you find patterns in buying or consumption that can aid in marketing or recommendation use cases. It will be of limited use in network security problems. You should become familiar with the general-purpose pattern discovery techniques, and then research specific techniques as you enter new domains.

Clustering

The most general-purpose technique for pattern discovery projects is clustering. As you are no doubt aware, clustering algorithms take your data and combine it with a metric for determining similarity between points and thereby generate an arrangement of those data points into clusters. Clustering is typically done to define a discrete set of clusters, but it can be used to produce a hierarchical diagram like the one shown in Figure 14.1.

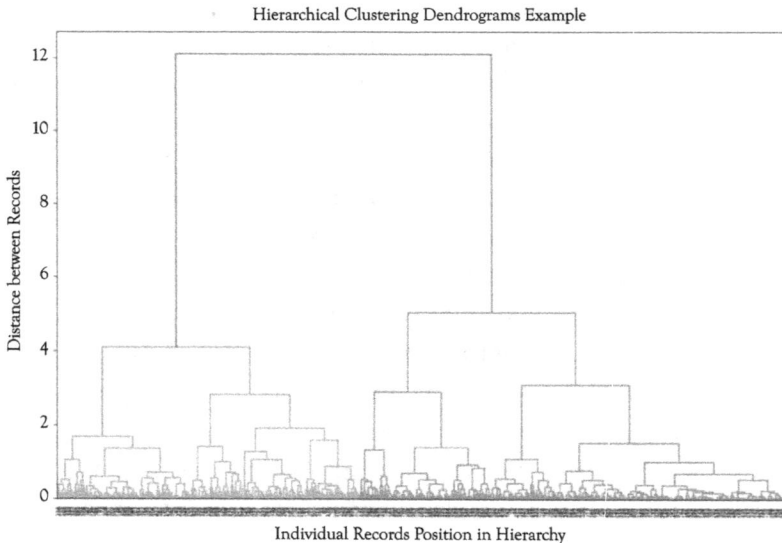

Figure 14.1 Hierarchical clustering example

Clustering can be applied in multiple ways to uncover patterns in data. Despite the general applicability of the technique, there are only three key levers you have at your disposal to guide the outcome:

1. The clustering algorithm you choose.
2. The similarity metric you use.
3. How you analyze the content of the clusters.

The choice of a clustering algorithm will depend on the number of features, the distribution of the data, and the expected structure and number of underlying groups. Simulation studies have suggested that overestimation of expected clusters tends to produce better results;[1] however, it would be fair to summarize the field by saying that in general algorithm choice resists reduction to simple heuristics. This means, as a general rule, you should experiment with multiple techniques for your project. A consequence of this is that you will need a very concrete idea about how you would differentiate a good outcome from a bad one. As you are investigating the data for patterns you have not seen before, making this distinction can be difficult. To make the task easier you should pay particular attention to how you measure similarity and analyze clusters.

Similarity Metrics

Defining similarity metrics is a difficult process, whatever choices you make are going to exert a bias over the kinds of patterns you can discover. In a very real sense, your capacity to conceive of what similarity means for a problem limits the outcomes of your investigation. For example, if you design a similarity metric for users of your website that is the number of identical pages they have looked at, then you are ignoring the device they use to look at the website and the time of day they are doing so. You are also ignoring the effect of the total amount of pages consumed. Such a metric emphasizes the overlap in content consumed while ignoring the way it is consumed.

It could be that your choice of the viewed pages metric provides the greatest separation of customers into those that just read the privacy policy before signing up versus those that just come to read the blog. Such a situation could reveal that the blog readers tend to be on mobile devices, while customers who sign-up tend to use desktop computers. However, if you clustered on the distribution of times of day, for when people browse the website you might discover that people browsing in the early evening

---

[1] M. Rodriguez, C.H. Comin, D. Casanova, O.M. Bruno, D.R. Amancio, L.F. Costa, and F.A. Rodrigues. January 15, 2019. "Clustering Algorithms: A Comparative Approach," *Plos ONE*. https://doi.org/10.1371/journal.pone.0210236

have a greater tendency to make a purchase, while those browsing during the day tend to have short visits to the website. In this hypothetical, we see that the metrics used to define similarity between system users will influence the patterns we find. These patterns are often very sensitive to the particulars of the similarity metric.

You can, of course, design a metric that includes many potential dimensions together. The problem is that there are numerous arbitrary decisions that need to be made in order to combine heterogenous data into a similarity metric. Many textbooks on these techniques simply talk about whether you use Euclidean, Manhattan, or some other distance metric. They presume that all data has been numerically encoded, and that the methods used to do the encoding are not open for consideration. In our example: There is no one right way to include shared pages viewed and time of day in a user similarity score.

For these reasons, it is worthwhile designing similarity metrics that are specific to the kinds of actionable scenarios you can imagine being taken. Or more importantly, metrics that are aligned with the kinds of actionable scenarios your business clients are prepared to take. As we discussed in earlier chapters, your client might have indicated that they are prepared to entertain any hypothesis, but that is rarely the case. The closer you can bring them to an analytical result that aligns with what they imagine a solution looking like, the greater the probability of success.

For example, if the marketing efforts of your company can be undertaken to target people based on their age and existing product holdings, then clustering on similarity of these will help you identify the commonalities and differences between the marketable groups of people. By embedding the known space of actions into the metric, you are increasing the likelihood that any insightful patterns are also actionable.

Cluster Members

The second critical aspect of applying clustering to business problems is determining what to do with the resulting clusters. If you have been able to define your similarity metric in a way that directly corresponds to potential actions, then this will not be a problem. If not, you will have clusters based on an ad-hoc combination of what data is available, what the client wants you to investigate and your own experimentation to try and find cleanly separated clusters.

Cleanly separated clusters are not in-and-of-themselves valuable. They may indicate natural partitions in the data, but they are not guaranteed to be actionable. They are also not necessarily explainable. To be useful, you need to find a way to explain the existence of these clusters in a way that is both understandable and actionable.

The standard approach is to identify some discerning features of the clusters that provide the actionable insight. For example, you might identify that one cluster contains people in the 45 to 65 age group with an existing credit card who are 10x more likely to take up life insurance than the general population, and 5x more likely than others of the same age group. The difficulty is that there are often many alternative factors that might distinguish between the members of your clusters. How do you determine what to look at? More importantly, the larger the number of potential variables you investigate, the more likely it is that you find a spurious pattern. Although there are statistical approaches to mitigating this multiple testing problem,[2] they require discipline and are difficult to explain to stakeholders.

The more you know about the kinds of actions the business is prepared to take, the more you can limit what you look at, and the greater confidence you can have in the patterns you find. If you must explore large numbers of potential causal factors (or actionable variables), then you need to be disciplined. This may sound like an obvious thing to say, but you need only look at the ongoing crisis of repeatability that is occurring in psychology and social science to understand that people can easily fall into bad statistical habits in the pursuit of a laudable outcome.[3]

What does it mean to be disciplined? It means plan out your analysis, work out what you are going to investigate, and what your acceptance criteria should be, given the scale of what you want to look at. Don't just do experiments until you get some results you are happy with and then

---

[2] W. Noble. 2009. "How Does Multiple Testing Correction Work?" *Nature Biotechnology* 27, no. 12, pp. 1135–1137.

[3] E. Yong. 2012. "Replication Studies: Bad Copy," *Nature* 485, pp. 298–300. https://doi.org/10.1038/485298a

share them with the client. If you cannot decide the entire scale upfront, then at the very least decide clearly the purpose of each individual experiment. If you are iterating and doing many of them, then always test for repeatability on an alternative data set.

Ideally, your entire process should be written in code that is structured such that repeating on different data or with different seeds can be easily automated. You do not want to be in the position of sharing an insight with a client only to discover it was a random pattern peculiar to the subset of data you looked at.

While everything I have just described may seem obvious, these kinds of problems are rife through large amounts of science and analytics, in the public and private sector. Regardless of the kinds of techniques that you employee, discipline is your best weapon against being fooled by randomness.

Beyond Clustering

Aside from clustering, there are other techniques that get used to do pattern discovery in data. Anomaly detection is another general-purpose technique that can be used across domains and data types. Many of the other techniques are specific to the kinds of data found in a given domain.

If the data has a natural network structure, such as customers, transactions, and merchants, then you can use various graph techniques to identify patterns in the network structure.[4] These kinds of algorithms can be used in fraud analysis to identify merchants where credit card numbers might be stolen or cloned.[5]

If you are looking at data sets with large amounts of text, then there are specific techniques for doing pattern discovery on text data. The field of topic modeling contains techniques that seek to identify distinct topics

---

[4] L. Akoglu, H. Tong, and D. Koutra. 2015. "Graph Based Aanomaly Detection and Description: A Survey," *Data Mining and Knowledge Discovery* 29, pp. 626–688.

[5] E. Kurshan, H. Shen, and H. Yu. 2020. "Financial Crime & Fraud Detection Using Graph Computing: Application Considerations & Outlook." Second International Conference on Transdisciplinary AI (TransAI).

or themes in a set of documents, the so-called latent or unobserved variables. The process is not entirely dissimilar from clustering, except that the similarity measurement is very specific to text data. In its most basic form, it involves an adaptation of the tf-idf algorithm in which you discover groups of words that commonly occur together and seem to be distinct to a subset of the documents.[6]

Whichever techniques you use for pattern discovery you will need to decide on criteria that are used to determine when a pattern is worthy of consideration for action. This is the Achilles heel of pattern discovery projects; it may seem convenient to launch into data analysis without careful consideration of what success looks like. But this is delaying the inevitable; at some point, you need to outline the criteria by which your results are deemed worthy of making them actionable.

Agents of Confirmation Bias

Before we conclude this chapter, it is important to discuss a common failing in pattern discovery projects. The difficulty of defining concrete success criteria upfront means that it is often delayed, and projects routinely adopt the pattern as follows:

1. The project is initiated on a specific data set with the open-ended goal of mining the data for useful patterns.
2. The data scientist engages in an iterative process of extracting patterns, visualizing them and attempting to explain them to stakeholders.
3. The sponsor absorbs these explanations, approves or disapproves of what they reveal, and then directs the next iteration of experimentation.
4. The process continues until the sponsor is satisfied with the results.

This pattern of behavior can have you playing the role of sculpting data until you have confirmed the biases of your sponsor. Most data scientists would find this kind of project frustrating and unrewarding. Usually this occurs because the sponsor is more assertive than the data scientist

---

[6] I. Vayansky, and S.A.P. Kumar. 2020. "A Review of Topic Modeling Methods," *Information Systems* 94. https://doi.org/10.1016/j.is.2020.101582

and simultaneously does not understand the statistical problems with this approach. The only solution is to be prescriptive about the process, explain the real possibility of spurious pattern discovery, outline rigorous processes to mitigate it, and push for objective success criteria.

Summary

Pure pattern discovery projects are interesting but risky endeavors. You can guarantee to deliver a report or analysis, but you cannot guarantee business impact. In most instances, you would better serve your client by steering the project toward something with more concrete goals and deliverables. There are certain problems and domains where pattern discovery commonly forms a critical part of a larger solution, fraud and security is one of these domains. By understanding how pattern discovery contributes to these solutions, we can more effectively apply it in other domains.

Clustering is the most general of all pattern discovery techniques and affords you multiple methods of adjusting it to your needs. You should consider carefully both how you measure similarity between records in your data, and the way you analyze the resulting clusters. For an introduction to pattern discovery techniques such as clustering and association rule mining, the reader is referred to the book *Business Intelligence and Data Mining.*[7]

---

[7] A.K. Maheshwari. 2015. *Business Intelligence and Data Mining* (New York, NY: Business Expert Press).

CHAPTER 15

Predictive Modeling

Predictive modeling tasks take many forms, but they all consist of problems where one or more variables that are critical to the organization need to be known before they can be measured. In some instances, the client may not have specifically asked for predictions of a specific variable, or even mentioned prediction. Regardless, there are certain key characteristics of a problem that clearly demarcate it as requiring a predictive model. These features are:

1. The problem requires acting before those key variables are measured.
2. The key variables are sufficient to determine the (probable) right course of action.
3. There are other data points available that appear related to the key variables.

Prediction projects occur when the proposed solution to the problem requires that you anticipate the value of these key variables to make a decision and take action. In this chapter, we will discuss some subtleties in the definition of prediction projects, the importance of clearly defined targets and alignment with potential actions. We will conclude the chapter with a discussion of the interface between predictive models and business processes so that you can tune and optimize your models for business outcomes.

Prediction or Detection

The focus on future events is what makes prediction different from general business analytics. In analytics, we focus on timely detection of changes and understanding the status quo so it can be acted upon. For example, if you need to detect when revenue is down for the month you are providing an analytical monitoring system. It is not explicitly predicting the future. If, however, you want to feed that revenue information into a model that anticipates the end-of-quarter result, then you are trying to predict something before it has happened.

The line between prediction and detection can be blurry and difficult for people to discriminate. In the previous example, the threshold for revenue drop might be seen as quite sensitive because the businesspeople using it are going to infer whether revenue for the whole month is in danger. They are themselves making predictions from the signal your system detects. The critical difference to keep at the forefront of your mind is where does the prediction explicitly occur? Does the system you are supplying detect signals that humans use for prediction? Or are you required to build something that explicitly makes the prediction for them?

The other common point of confusion is whether the thing being predicted needs to be in the future. Some predictive models are used to predict things that have already happened, arguably some fraud detection models are predicting whether the transaction that just happened is fraudulent or not. The key discerning factor is not whether the event occurs in the future, but whether the measurement does. If you are able to measure something directly in the moment, then you don't need a prediction. If you need to wait for measurement to occur, then prediction can add value to the process.

Clear Target Variables

We commonly refer to the variable being predicted as the target variable, but you should be aware that in the statistics community it is also known as the dependent variable. The identity of the target variable (or variables) should be very clear from your initial interviews and the data you have seen. For example, you should have an un-ambiguous way to define which customers have used a stolen card, or which ones have churned, or which ones have canceled their subscription, and so on. If this target variable is not well defined, then you need to make it clear to your client that this is a requirement.

If your client cannot tell you how to identify the target events from their own data, then you need to stop the project and rewind to the discussion of measurement. You will likely need to engage in a process of working with the client to define a method for measuring or estimating the real-world quantity that the business cares about. It is critical that this is done in consultation with the client. They need to be on that journey with you and sign-off on the chosen method for defining the target variable. Do not move forward with modeling until you have shown them data about what this target variable says about the problem (numbers per month, trend over time, demographic breakdown, etc.). When your client has signed off on the target variable, then you can move into trying to predict it.

Target and Action Alignment

It is not uncommon for a client to have decided in advance what they want to predict. They may be enthralled by the idea of doing predictive modeling and have themselves scoped out what the project should consist of. It is important that you review the target variable and its relationship to the intended action.

The client may have decided what needs to be predicted based on the data they have historically used for analyzing the problem. Deeper questioning might reveal that the data isn't used in its raw form. They may transform it, or cherry pick through it, using unwritten rules. It may not be the only resource used when decisions are being made and actions taken. What this means is that the proposed model might only solve part of the problem.

For example, I have been given projects in which the stated goal is to forecast revenue, and in so doing identify correlated variables that can be used as crucial industry indicators. This sounds like a perfectly reasonable request. In these situations, additional questions often reveal that the decisions to be made and the impacts they have are not uniformly distributed. For example, it may be more important to get an indication that revenue is likely to take a dive in the next six months, than it is to know that it will grow at slightly above average rates for the next six months. The reason is that the first scenario requires an intervention, whereas the second does not.

Why is this?

The reason is that the value of a prediction is generally not constant across all the potential outputs that a model might produce. It is often far more important to know when something is going to go wrong, than when it will continue as normal. In this case, we might want to rephrase the problem from a pure regression (predict revenue in the next quarter) to a classification or probability estimate problem. For example, what is the probability that in the next quarter the revenue will be lower than 90 percent of the budgeted value?

In this example, we are completely redefining the focus of the model building to better suit the desired course of action. We still have a prediction problem, but we have reframed the target variable so that it is in alignment with the action that will be taken. The new target variable means the model does not need to identify the timing and volume of the market peaks, because that is not when action will be taken. The art of identifying opportunities to reframe like this, in fact the essence of building a useful model, requires that you identify the imbalances in the value of information.

Like many of the issues we are discussing this is easier said than done. The key to identifying these imbalances is knowing how the predictions will be acted upon and knowing what the expected impact of those actions would be. This needs to include the cost of inaction when certain key states come to be, even when they were not predicted. In essence, you need a map that outlines all the states of the world that the client says they are trying to anticipate, how they would act in each instance, and then the value/cost of being right or wrong about each of them. Once you know the relative value of all possible outcomes, you can meaningfully discuss what should be the target variable for a model, how to approach the problem, and how to tune and apply the model.

Classification Problems

In the previous example of revenue forecasting, we declared that the only value came from knowing about movements downward. That was the only prediction that the business intended to act on. This is a simplification of what many real-world scenarios involve, but it allows us to explore some of the core issues in classification problems.

We have so far only considered the impact of what we want to predict. We have not discussed the ways in which we could be wrong. If we ask the client what the costs are of the various combinations of outcomes and predictions, then we can tabulate the results. In Table 15.1, we provide a qualitative illustration for our where the drop in expected revenue is all we are trying to predict. This type of diagram is typically called a *cost matrix* in machine learning.[1]

Table 15.1 Example of cost/benefits of binary model

Prediction	Reality	Cost
No-Drop	No-Drop	None
No-Drop	Drop	Very High
Drop	No-Drop	Minor
Drop	Drop	None

In our hypothetical scenario, we have proposed that action is only taken when a drop is forecasted. Furthermore, we assume that when the forecast is correct the action (or inaction) results in a perfect outcome. So, in this scenario, there are only costs involved with being wrong. In truth, it might cost something when you predict a drop and act upon it. It is just that when it really does drop then you did the right thing, so making the prediction and acting on it has not cost you in relative terms because that drop was happening regardless of your actions. Or in other words the outcome could not have been better, hence no cost is assigned to that scenario.

In the other two scenarios, we see that being ignorant about a drop that occurs is very costly, whereas predicting a drop that does not occur results in only minor costs (the costs of taking unnecessary action). The false positives are far less of a concern than the false negatives. This may not be the case; it could be that taking unnecessary action is almost as costly as not acting when a real drop occurs. These are empirical matters that require the input of the client to settle.

---

[1] N. Nikolaou, N. Edakunni, M. Kull, P. Flach, and G. Brown. 2016. "Cost-Sensitive Boosting Algorithms: Do We Really Need Them?" *Machine Learning* 104, pp. 359–384.

The relative sizes of these four costs will tell you the expected impact of a given model. We can either try and incorporate this knowledge into the objective function used by the learning algorithm or we can calibrate the way the model is used based on this knowledge. This calibration usually takes the form of choosing an output threshold to use with the model.

Note, that at least one of the squares in a cost matrix should generally have a value of zero in it. This will be the square whose prediction results in no action, and the prediction is correct. In our previous example this is the no-drop, no-drop square. If your client provides a cost/benefit for all squares, then either the table contains the results of multiple actions, or they have made a mistake. Not doing anything under the right circumstances should have no cost or benefit associated with it. You should ask them to break down how each of those costs and benefits are realized. This will help you identify whether there are multiple actions being proposed, or if the client has mistakenly assigned costs/benefits that should not be present.

Your client may argue that the situation of correctly not acting should be considered a benefit, because the existing process causes them to take unnecessary actions. This is a mistake; they are conflating evaluating the current process with evaluating the model. These two calculations should be done separately, so that you can clearly see the net gain with using the model compared to the status quo.

The type of confusion described in the last paragraph results from a lack of clarity about how to analyze the impact of decision making with a model. In our example, we focused on the costs of making mistakes. We did this because the reference point for the analysis was revenue behaving as expected in the budget. This was the neutral point against which costs could be avoided or incurred. In many instances, we might analyze the impact as benefits relative to some other baseline. For example, if the company wanted to know when revenue would exceed certain levels, enabling them to make choices about inventory or cash reserve management.

In the majority of problems, there is a symmetry between a cost-based analysis and a benefit-based analysis. For example, a customer churn model can be analyzed as reducing the costs of churning customers, or as the benefit of retaining customers who would otherwise have left. In these instances, you cannot do the analysis using both costs and benefits because to do so involves double counting the impact of potential churn events. This is usually transparent, because the values of the costs and the benefits are perfectly symmetrical. For example, the cost of a lost customer is $10,000 in forgone revenue, and the benefit is $10,000 in retained revenue. Having both values in your cost/benefit analysis involves double counting. Consider the situation when a single instance moves from being a false negative to a true positive. In this cast, a cost of $10,000 is removed and a benefit of $10,000 is added. The net effect is $20,000 on the analysis, thus illustrating that you are double counting these impacts.

In some rare cases you can do both cost and benefit analysis simultaneously, this occurs when these impacts are independent of each other. For example, if we modify our revenue forecasting example to be a forecast on the price of an asset. We could benefit from forecasting a drop by shorting that asset (as well as moving our portfolio into other securities). However, the cost of not forecasting a drop is the loss of value in our position. In this case there are additional benefits of correctly forecasting the event, beyond just mitigation of the costs of the event.

In this section, we have focused on a binary decision with correspondence to a binary classification model. It is worth noting that the correspondence need not always hold. It is possible to make a binary decision based on a multiclass classification model, as well as to take multiple decisions on the basis of binary classification models. The key lesson of this section is to map out the potential decisions and outcomes and use them to think clearly about how to build and optimize your model.

Regression Models

In the previous section, we discussed a situation in which the client expressed a desire to forecast revenue. It was then decided that they were only interested in knowing when it would drop by a certain amount. This allowed us to transform a regression problem into a classification problem. If the model is intended to be used for a single binary decision, then this is an ideal outcome. We can switch focus to predicting the one thing the client actually cares about rather than trying to model the entire process. Unfortunately, some projects cannot be transformed in this way. Certain problems demand that what is delivered is a regression model that predicts the value of some quantity critical to the business.

In general, estimating the potential impact of a regression model is considerably harder. To see why cast your mind back to the outcomes we discussed previously. By transforming the problem to binary classification, we reduced the number of situations we need to consider when evaluating a model. We looked at the costs/benefits of being right or wrong under the two possible forecasts. A grand total of four situations needed to be evaluated. We could use these values to inform the modeling process and evaluate the potential ROI of any model we produce.

A model that produces a real valued forecast is somewhat more difficult to evaluate from a decision theoretic perspective. You can be wrong by varying degrees, and either too high or too low. There may be different costs/benefits associated with different magnitudes and directions of the error. The structure of these costs/benefits depends on the decision landscape and may be influenced by the specific values of the prediction and real target value. All of these complications mean that there are no general processes for determining the business effectiveness of a pure regression model. There are only standard metrics for evaluating the predictive performance of the model.

There are some industries in which the business case analysis of a model is well developed. Not surprisingly, insurance is on the top of this list, owing to the fact that their entire business is built on top of estimating risks and costs. How do they evaluate their regression models in insurance? One of the approaches is relatively straightforward. They have a model for the likelihood of a claim being made, and they have a regression model of the costs when a claim is made. The model's projected costs of a taking on a particular policy can be calculated from these two estimates. As a business they get to choose which applications they can accept, and the mixture of policies they have on their book determines the total expected costs over a period of time. Insurance companies work toward better models of risks and expected costs, but given any particular model the key lever they have is whether to accept or reject an application.

The power of the actuarial approach is that they are directly modeling financial impacts, combining risks and costs to get expected business outcome. Given a history of accepted policies and their outcomes, they can simulate the impact of an alternative model. In other words, they can test a regression model combined with decision criteria against historical data to determine whether the results are favorable. In this sense, their evaluation of a model is a direct simulation of the financial impact of having used that model. A similar process is used in quantitative finance called a backtest of a model.

Unfortunately, many data science projects do not involve building models of the business benefits or costs directly. So, the actuarial approach is not available to us. Conceivably, you can always make the argument to your client that the project would be improved by modeling the business outcome directly. However, your client may not have an appetite such an undertaking. Instead, we are often tasked with forecasting something that will be used for a variety of decisions or fed into other systems. The actual impact of the forecast on those other systems is left to you to model or evaluate as best as you can.

To understand the difficulty of evaluating these models, it is worthwhile considering some examples. Take systems that work in optimizing assignment of ad inventory. Typically, each ad slot is time limited, and some action always needs to be taken. If an ad is not assigned then revenue is lost, regardless of whether the assigned ad is optimal or not.

If your company needs to forecast something about an ad slot before deciding which ad to show (number of viewers, demographic profile, expected conversions, etc.), then that forecast needs to be used for every event. Action is always taken, and the model is always involved. The decisions might involve hard thresholds that determine among options. However, you still need to do something with all the cases that do not meet any of the thresholds. Given this complexity, it is reasonable to ask how we can achieve the same robust evaluation of costs and benefits that is possible for binary decisions.

The first key criterion is to understand how the real value of the prediction influences the decision. Is the relationship a series of thresholds that determine whether particular actions are taken? Or is the value of prediction quantitatively involved in the decision? In the case of the former, we might find that no matter how complex the problem seems, it can be broken down into a series of binary decisions. When we start to write down the costs and benefits, we will find that the cells relate to specific actions (with associated costs and benefits). Other costs will be in another table, because additional criteria are used to determine the action.

This will provide us with a cascading series of decisions and cost matrices, a simple example of which is shown in Figure 15.1.

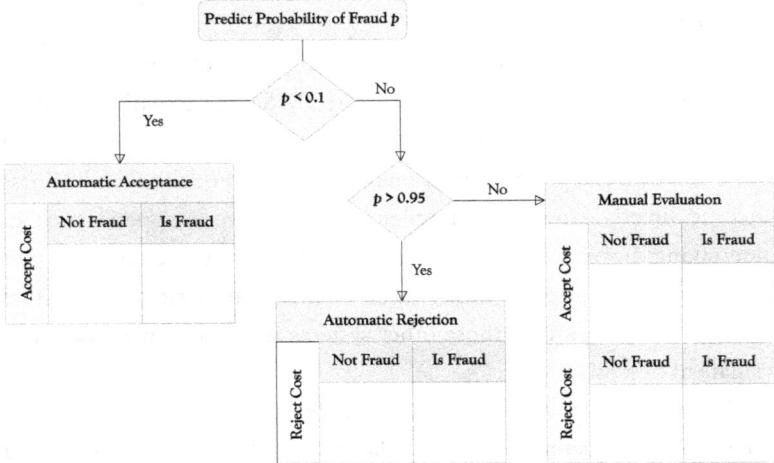

Figure 15.1 Multidecision cost matrix example

A regression model that can be analyzed for its influence over a series of binary decisions could potentially be reframed as a series of binary classifiers. There are complications, because you will need to think about the true sampling population for building each model. However you approach it, the assignment of costs and benefits through a series of binary decisions makes the procedure for evaluating the business impact of the model straightforward.

If the model is not being used for binary decisions, then you need to understand how the prediction influences the specific actions. One key aspect is to understand whether that analysis can be done in terms of individual errors or across populations. By which I mean, are the predictions used individually, or is their influence exerted through an aggregation of predictions. Let me illustrate what I mean with an anecdote.

When I worked on models to forecast the number of viewers for a broadcast television station, I initially built models that were evaluated using standard metrics, such as mean absolute error (MAE) and mean squared error (MSE). These metrics are averages of performance across the individual predictions.

As I got further into the project, it became clear that the aggregate error was what was important, because broadcast inventory is never sold in individual slots. A client buys a campaign consisting of large numbers of ad slots. Ultimately, what they care about is that they reach a cumulative audience target in their desired demographic category. This means that a model with a larger MAE could conceivably be a better model if that error was closer to being perfectly distributed around zero for the subset of purchased inventory.

A regression model can be used to take an action that involves aggregated predictions. This situation means that the estimator bias (or mean error) of the model is potentially more important than any other metric. By monitoring the mean error, we monitor the expected error over random aggregations of the predictions.

Further into the project it became clear that this approach was also imperfect, for the following reason. Inventory for a given campaign is not chosen randomly from the pool. First, it is usually chosen from a constrained time period (four to six weeks); second, it is often region specific, and quite often restricted to certain categories of media or times of day. This means that in an ideal world I would have been monitoring the distribution of error across large numbers of overlapping subsets in the data. In all of which I needed the error distributed evenly around zero, with as small as possible magnitude.

If it were possible to specify upfront what all the desired subsets are (and it is generally not), then you could in principle write a single expression that gives you a metric for the error of a given model. You would soon discover that, just like in the previous example, not all the subsets of inventory have equal value. Some are in higher demand than others and hence lower error is of greater importance. Again, there is nothing in principle stopping you from seeking explicit weightings for all these things and writing it up in one big expression.

We should stop at this point and reflect on the feasibility of what we are trying to do. We are trying to understand how to measure the optimal model where the predictions will be used within variable-sized overlapping subsets of forecasts that have varying impact on the business. In most instances this endeavor will fail. It will fail because obtaining all this information will be hard, and because you will generally find that there are always additional considerations you have not yet quantified.

You may be tempted to argue that the business owners should know all these details. Data scientists tend to overestimate the extent to which businesspeople understand their businesses quantitatively. The behavioral economist Richard Thaler provides an interesting discussion of a similar phenomenon in the history of economics. It was thought for a long time that rational businesspeople determined production quotas and pricing through something called marginal analysis. It turned out that in practice businesspeople tend not to behave the way economists think they do. Many decisions made by businesspeople are done either by instinct or by following simple heuristics like maximize sales, irrespective of revenue.[2]

The lesson for data scientists is that even though we are driving to design systems that optimize business processes, we should not expect that our stakeholders will know all the quantitative metrics that we might think they should. We should accept that it may be infeasible to map out all of the fine details that will determine the impact of our regression models. Given this, how do we make good decisions in the design and development of a solution? There are two key ideas widely used in the sciences that study complex systems that we can borrow for many use cases: simplified models and simulation.

Simplified Models

Through much of history a simplified model was the only option for dealing with complex systems. The simple model is designed such that it maintains the core drivers of the behavior you are investigating. In this approach, I am suggesting you design a model of business impact that you know is a simplification of the real process but contains what you expect to be the key elements.

Instead of trying to parameterize every aspect of the business process, you ask for the dominant factors and quantification of their influence. You delve into how these would be impacted by the error distribution of

---

[2] R.H. Thaler. 2015. *Misbehaving, The Making of Behavioral Economics* (Penguin Books), p. 88.

your candidate regression model. You can do the same thing for multiple models and look at the relationships between standard machine learning metrics and the estimated business impact. You can then discuss some scenarios with your client. A simplified model has the added advantage that you should be able to explain it to the client and feel that they will understand what you have done.

Note, we are talking here about a simplified model of the business impact, not necessarily a simplified predictive model. It gives you a replacement for reporting MAE or MSE of a model and allows you to report an estimate of economic impact. By iteratively adding more complexity to the business model, you can test for stability and seek feedback from that client on the quality of the estimates produced.

Simulation

The second option for achieving estimates of business impact is simulation. In the study of complex systems like weather and climate, computer simulation is a standard technique for gaining insights into how changes can ripple through a system. Much like the first option, you will need to build models that are simplifications. However, in the first instance you are using a simplified deterministic model of the business impact directly. In the simulation instance you will be modeling how the business behaves, then using that model to simulate the impact of introducing a given predictive model or decision-making process.

Aside from a method of modeling the business process, you will also need to build a simulation tool, with assumptions expressed as parameters. The simulation tool should operate on a backtested regression forecast with the known errors it made over the backtest period. It can then simulate the business process using that model for decisions and evaluate the impact of those predictions with their observed errors. Typically, these simulations are run over a suite of different assumptions, allowing you to test the sensitivity of the business impact to the conditions expressed in the assumptions.

A simulation like this, while initially harder to explain to business-people, will give them an opportunity to understand the complexity of evaluating the error in the model. You can show them how the outcome changes with certain parameters. The parameters of your simulation may determine how the model is applied; for example, the threshold used from a scoring function for choosing which customers to target. Alternatively, there may be parameters that describe assumptions that have been made about the business operations (average customer lifetime, average transaction amount, etc.). Another alternative is that the parameters embody assumptions about the business and economic environment. All these types of parameters can be varied, allowing simulations to be run under a variety of scenarios.

Writing and running simulation software has the added benefit of illustrating which of the assumptions and parameters matter. It may be that certain parameters have minimal impact on the outcomes, while others can make it vary wildly. This will help you work with the business to identify what it is they need to know before deploying their regression model.

Neither of the two suggestions I have made here are entirely satisfying. When compared with the robust kind of analysis you can make for binary classifier, it is somewhat frustrating that regression models do not always lend themselves to a similar business case analysis. It would be preferable to make strong claims about how a model will impact a business, rather than having to resort to simplifications and simulations to estimate the impact. You can console yourself with the knowledge that even receiver operating characteristic (ROC) analysis is a simulation of sorts. It generally assumes that the business environment and the distributions of all data will remain unchanged, and that is rarely if ever the case.

Summary

Effective prediction modeling requires data sets with accurate and reliable target variables to predict. In addition, these target variables need to have a meaningful relationship with the decisions and actions that a business will take to solve a problem. While investigating these two critical requirements, you need to analyze how the model will be used in decision making. This process will start you down the path to understanding the potential ROI of the model and may even allow you to tweak the design of a solution or model to optimize that ROI.

For an introduction to predictive modeling techniques with examples using a variety of open source and proprietary software packages, the reader is referred to *Data Mining Models* by David Olson.[3] For an introduction to the theoretical underpinnings of machine learning techniques, the reader is referred to *The Elements of Statistical Learning* by Jerome H. Friedman, Robert Tibshirani, and Trevor Hastie.[4]

---

[3] D.L. Olson. 2018. *Data Mining Models* (New York, NY: Business Expert Press), 2nd ed.
[4] J.H. Friedman, R. Tibshirani, and T. Hastie. 2017. *The Elements of Statistical Learning* (Springer), 2nd ed.

CHAPTER 16

Model Context

Once you are convinced that your prediction project has a target variable that is aligned to the actions or decisions that will be taken, you are in position to begin modeling. In the previous chapter, we explored some ways that an understanding of the costs and benefits could influence your modeling. In this chapter, we will explore other factors to keep at the front of your mind in the modeling process. Many of these topics have already been raised in previous chapters. They are here because these details are easy to forget in your enthusiasm for applying a particular technique.

Timing Is Everything

Be sure you have a solid grasp of the timing of various factors in the problem scenario. Timing can influence how you engineer features, how you structure the training data and the models you choose. You should be aware of what it takes to prepare data for scoring, and how long it will take to train a model. In extreme cases, large complex models can take so long to train that the data they are trained on is already stale by the time it is deployed.

There is a trade-off between building a better model and getting it into operation late, versus a simple (and a little dirtier model) that is brought into production quickly. The critical consideration is the sensitivity of the problem to using a model that is trained on old data. A consideration here is whether your model can bootstrap from previous iterations of the same model or be built from a generic or partially trained model that can be fine-tuned on the latest available data. Neural networks, for example, are so good at making reuse of previous solutions that they have spawned a subfield that looks at ways they can transfer what is learned across problems and domains.[1]

---

[1] S.J. Pan , and Q. Yang. 2010. "A Survey on Transfer Learning," *IEEE Transactions on Knowledge and Data Engineering* 22, no. 10, pp. 1345–1359.

Scaling Up

Further to the consideration of timing, we should consider how the problem will scale as time progresses. It is possible to choose a model that works well on the initial data sets, but as the customer base grows, or data warehouse starts to fill up, you might find it struggling to process requests. If the training or scoring time scales poorly, then at some point you will need to change models.

A method of side-stepping the scaling problem is to only ever use the most recent subset of your data. You determine the amount of data that the learning algorithm can handle and then use that amount. However, this decision does not solve the scaling of growing records to score, and it may have an impact on model performance. It has been a widely reported observation that more data tends to trump fancier algorithms;[2] hence, you should at the very least be testing the potential performance gains of using all available data with algorithms that can use it effectively.

It may seem premature to consider how the model will scale when the project is just at the beginning. The time it takes to complete a model, deploy it, and embed it into the necessary systems necessitates that you consider scaling factors. You can easily investigate many aspects of the scaling through careful experimentation. How does performance of the model scale with more data? How does training and scoring time scale with more data? How fast is the production data set growing? How does the performance of a simpler model scale with data? If you answer these questions, then you can anticipate when problems might occur in a production system. You will be able to make recommendations based on how long a model needs to be in operation before being replaced.

Designing a deployment architecture for a machine learning model involves thinking about what is required now, as well as planning for what will be required a year or two from now. I will discuss this topic in a later chapter, but it is worth stressing (in case it is not obvious) that decisions you make at the modeling stage have ramifications when it comes to deployment.

---

[2] A. Halevy, P. Norvig, and F. Pereira. 2009. "The Unreasonable Effectiveness of Data," *Intelligent Systems* 24, pp. 8–12. IEEE.

Understanding the Outputs

Sometimes clients want to understand what the numerical outputs of a model mean. This understanding can be required to sign off on the work, or because a human will be included in the production system and needs to interpret the output in order to make decisions or take an action. In many instances, the outputs will be transparent. You could be predicting a label for the data or forecasting the number of widgets that will be sold. But this interpretation is not so easy if you are building a quantile regression or a ranking model.

Models that naturally produce a probability estimate are on the cusp of being understandable. You cannot assume that because the notion of predicting a probability is comprehensible to you, that it will be to your clients. Take the time to talk with them about what a probability means. Ensure they are comfortable with designing business rules based on probabilities. If the client is not comfortable working with probabilities, then you can explore using an odds-based risk score (commonly used in finance[3]), or a matrix-based risk score (commonly used in health[4]).

Some modeling techniques will produce seemingly arbitrary scores that effectively rank the input data. These models are generally more difficult to explain. You can endeavor to fit probability distributions to the model after it is built using techniques such as Platt Scaling or Isotonic Regression.[5] However, it is worthwhile knowing if this will be a requirement well in advance. You are generally better off doing the modeling with the goal of producing well-calibrated probabilities, rather than trying to tack them on at the end.

---

[3] T. Liu. 2019. "Intro to Credit Scorecard," *Blog Post.* https://towardsdatascience .com/intro-to-credit-scorecard-9afeaaa3725f

[4] J. Li, B. Chunbing, and D. Wu. 2018. "How to Design Rating Schemes of Risk Matrices: A Sequential Updating Approach," *Risk Analysis* 38, pp. 99–117.

[5] A. Niculescu-Mizil, and R. Caruana. August 2005. "Predicting Good Probabilities With Supervised Learning," *ICML '05: Proceedings of the 22nd international conference on Machine learning*, pp. 625–632. https://doi.org/10.1145/1102351.1102430

Model Interpretability

Your client may also require that the model you produce provides some level of transparency into how it processes data to produce its output. Clients are often concerned with more than just what the output means, they might want to understand what the inputs mean, and what is involved in producing the output.

Your client will likely not explicitly state that they want model interpretability, much less the specific techniques they want applied. It will be up to you to understand the level of explanation they require, and find an appropriate technique, or choose an appropriate model. There are a variety of questions your client might ask to indicate they have interpretability requirements:

"Can we see what is driving customer churn?"
"What would happen if we changed the price?"
"Are there regional differences in customer churn?"
"Can we see if the model is making a biased or unfair decision?"
"Can we test the impact of a new store?"
"What can the model tell me about our customers?"
"How can I be certain the model is accurate?"

The last of these concerns is more common than people in our industry care to admit. You do not have to look very hard to find someone who does not trust mathematics. Irrespective of whether you feel their mistrust to be justifiable or not, you will still need to help them make use of your analysis. For this reason, it is worthwhile to take on their frame of mind (deep distrust of the model) and look for ways to engender trust, and simultaneously enable intuitive insight.

There are many techniques for showing how models work and what drives them. The entire field of model explainability and interpretability is developing rapidly. Rather than summarize this moving target, I am going to outline two general-purpose approaches for gaining trust and understanding of your models. These will be As-if Charts that introduce backtests, and What-if Analysis that allows the client to do manual sensitivity analysis.

As-If Chart

One way to create trust in your models is to demonstrate outcomes as-if the model was already being used. The idea is to apply the model to data from specific historical slices, and then plot results against known outcomes. In other words, create a chart by plotting historical data alongside predictions or confidence intervals from a model trained on data up to that point in time.

In our field we routinely do these backtests to check that our model is viable, but it is likely to be a novel idea for your client. Explain how you are only using data available up to a given point in the past to build the model and then simulate how it would have performed on data after that point. The As-if Chart will show your client what the predictions would have been had they already been using your model. It will simultaneously encourage trust in the model (if that trust is justified) and it may show the client if there are certain scenarios in which the model is systematically better or worse.

This task is simple if the data is time series. If you have some other data, like customer conversions or churn, then you will need to come up with creative ways of plotting. You should always start by emphasizing the out-of-time nature of the test. For example, plot the proportion of customers predicted to churn versus the proportion that did, over time. Demonstrate how the model would be effective over time.

You will likely need to go deeper to satisfy the client's requirement to understand what the model is doing. For example, first take the customers in the out-of-time slice and break them into segments that the client finds intuitive (regions, accounts, and products). You can then show the predictive accuracy of the model on each segment alone, or across multiple time slices plotted sequentially.

The process of plotting against time helps the client understand they are looking at a simulation of what will happen when the model goes into production. Any other dimensions you add will help them understand what drives the model, and where its strengths or weaknesses might be.

What-If Analysis

One way people gain an understanding of something new is via probing and testing. By making changes and observing outcomes, people obtain a sense of the underlying causal structure. This is so important that it has been found to be part of childhood development. Children will conceive of interventions in self-directed play that becomes more efficient for learning causal structure as they develop cognitively.[6]

You can exploit this pathway of learning by creating applications over a predictive model that allow your stakeholders to experiment with it. As they alter the values of the input parameters, they can see how it affects the predictions that are made. The key idea is to encourage familiarity with how the model makes its predictions through interaction, rather than consuming static plots.

The process of interacting and experimenting with the model might allow the client to learn intuitions like the following:

Regardless of what the other values are, once a customer reaches the age of 55 the probability of churn is always over 50 percent

Or

Our female customers are consistently less likely not to churn than the males with the same demographic features.

If you have any doubt that interaction is an intuitive way to learn how something works, then ask yourself the following: How often do I read instruction manuals? Building interactive tools will take more time than most projects allow, but if you are able to invest the energy in a reusable tool of some kind you will find it a valuable method for helping your clients develop intuitions and trust.

---

[6] T. McCormack, N. Bramley, C. Frosch, F. Patrick, and D. Lagnado. 2016. "Children's Use of Interventions to Learn Causal Structure," *Journal of Experimental Child Psychology* 141, pp. 1–22. https://doi.org/10.1016/j.jecp.2015.06.017

Summary

We have discussed several considerations that should be top of mind in the modeling process. All of which are a common source of problems later in a project. You want to be sure that the model you propose putting into production can function within the time constraints of the business. You need to be sure that it will scale with the business over a reasonable time frame. You want to have an idea of how you are going to explain your model such that stakeholders will be comfortable with what it is doing and trust it enough to move to production.

CHAPTER 17

Project Delivery

Once you have weighed up all the requirements of the project and decided how to approach your analysis and experimentation, all that remains is to get it done. Despite the almost infinite diversity of what your delivery could entail, there are a number of principles that always make the process efficient. These guiding principles make delivering data science easier and more likely to succeed. In this chapter, we will discuss factors internal to your process (version control, documentation, Notebook discipline, and data management) and factors that relate to management of external factors (client check-in meetings and the migration to production).

Version Control

Version control refers to a family of software applications that allow you to maintain a history of changes to your code and collaborate with others. There are multiple options available, although Git appears to have built a large usage lead over the other tools, as it is at the top of the list of most used developer tools in the most recent Stack Overflow Survey.[1]

In all likelihood, you will have had some exposure to Git through the free repository hosting service GitHub (acquired by Microsoft). There are other hosting services available, all of which tend to offer you some level of service for free, allowing you to store copies of your code in a project on their servers. Although companies previously hosted their own version control servers, usage of the online services is becoming universally adopted. If you are not already familiar with Git, you can use these services to create and manipulate a toy project to learn how to save and update code using Git.

---

[1] Stack Overflow. 2021. "Developer Survey." https://insights.stackoverflow.com/survey/2021

If your client does not use version control, then you should suggest it. If the code and data are sensitive, then the repository may need to reside within their internal network. For most projects you should be able to convince them to host the code in a private cloud-based repository.

To fully realize the benefits of using a version control system you need to integrate it into your work process. You should be aiming to continually check your work into the repository. This will mean your work is continually backed up and you can easily return to previous versions if you make a mistake. There are multiple styles of working with version control, which depend on what you are building and who you are working with. There are several key ideas that are widely adopted: make use of *Tags* to identify key milestones in the project and use *branches* to maintain independent streams of work that will need to be integrated at some point.

The benefits of using version control extend beyond merely ensuring your code is safe. If you incorporate it into your experimention and development process and use it daily, then you are imposing a natural rhythm on your progress. Forcing yourself to push into a repository will encourage you to write code in neat, self-contained blocks. If your progress is less clean, then you can simply push changes you are making into a branch until you have a completed block of running code.

One word of warning, all source control tools have their idiosyncrasies, and it is possible to get your code into a messy state. Be sure to take the time to understand the problems that can occur with your chosen tool. I can almost guarantee that you will sometime find yourself in a state where you feel like you have lost some work. There are two rules for avoiding major loss of work when you are still learning to use a version control system:

A. Know what action you should be taking regularly in order to be able to save work. In the world of Git, this means add, commit, and push your changes. Learn that sequence and use it religiously.

B. Before you merge your work with other people's make a manual backup. This sounds backward and might draw laughter from experienced software engineers. However, until you can safely say you have mastered your version control system, it is the only way to ensure you don't lose work or get your project into an unmanageable state. Merging is usually where disasters occur, so back up before you do it. I have several times felt that I was comfortable with the tools, not followed my own advice and ended up regretting it.

Lab Books

Successful scientists have used journals for centuries. Allowing them to keep meticulous notes on everything they do, as they are doing it. The process of writing down your experiments allows you to keep track of what has been done and facilitates the replication of results. The process of documentation is important because data science also involves testing large numbers of ideas, and sometimes we do not recognize success until weeks or months after an experiment. Without adequate notes, an experiment may not be repeatable.

The reality of working in code and scripts has tended to make data scientists lax about writing documentation. There is a sense in which we feel our work is self-documenting. However, very often we are rewriting and overwriting scripts on a regular basis, iterating on what we have done. It is common for there to be manual steps taken in the process of munging data as it is prepared for downstream processes. For these reasons repeatability is still a common problem, because in most cases you cannot recapitulate history from the code base alone.

The delusion of believing in self-documenting code not only harms us through reduced repeatability but it also denies us the opportunity to use writing as an extension of thinking. There is considerable evidence that writing as a process contributes to the development of critical thinking,[2] as well as maintaining attention and facilitating information synthesis.[3]

---

[2] I.J. Quitadamo, and M.J. Kurtz. 2007. "Learning to Improve: Using Writing to Increase Critical Thinking Performance in General Education Biology," *CBE life sciences education* 6, no 2, pp. 140–154. doi:10.1187/cbe.06-11-0203
[3] J. Willis. July 11, 2011. "The Brain-Based Benefits of Writing for Math and Science Learning," *Edutopia Blog Post*. www.edutopia.org/blog/writing-executive-function-brain-research-judy-willis

Writing is likely not just a didactic tool; many people have observed that the process of writing bootstraps our thinking by allowing us to see the flaws in our thoughts as they are manifest on the page. This perspective has been perfectly encapsulated in the quote from historian and author David McCullough.

> Writing is thinking. To write well is to think clearly. That's why it's so hard.[4]

Your work will benefit if you take the time to write out the purpose and method of each experiment you conduct. Put them into separate scripts and use an overall project README file to navigate through the project. It is worthwhile making an update of the README part of your daily process.

Ideally, each experiment should have additional notes on any steps that were taken that are not scripted as code. It is also generally ideal to make notes about things you tried that failed and why the various scripts have been changed. This kind of note taking allows your experiments to be closer to repeatability, without forcing you to write everything you do into a single executable script.

It would be ideal if your README or notes contain references to tags used in your source control commits. This allows you to check out a code base as it was at the specific point in time when you ran the experiment. If you are making use of a shared set of library functions, then being able to return to previous versions also helps with reproducibility.

The core idea here is that documentation should never be treated as a post project house cleaning responsibility. Documentation helps with the process of doing data science by facilitating clear thinking and planning. Comprehensive documentation means better work, fewer mistakes, and an ability to easily revisit experimental threads when needed.

---

[4] D. McCullough. July/August 2002. "Interview with NEH chairman Bruce Cole," *Humanities* 23, no. 4. Transcript available at https://sagamoreinstitute.org/david-mccullough-on-teaching-citizenship/

Notebook Discipline

Some readers will be puzzled by the preceding discussion of documentation as they are already in the habit of using some form of Notebook application for embedding code and documentation together. Notebook servers, such as Jupyter[5] or Apache Zepplin,[6] provide a software architecture for creating artifacts that mix blocks of code and documentation. This allows the users to add documentation cells around core sections of code, and usually any plots and visualizations are embedded into the document. The entire artifact can be saved into a Git repository, and then viewed without requiring reexecution. All of which makes them excellent methods for preservation of experiments.

The data science community appears to have become dominated by Notebook-based development (as is reflected by multiple companies building data science integrated development environments (IDEs) inside Notebook servers). However, there are disadvantages to the use of Notebooks that you should be aware of so that you limit their impact on your projects. These disadvantages of Notebooks are in the repeatability of experiments, code reuse, and ease of deployment.

The repeatability problem of Notebooks lies in the spaghetti style execution model. Users typically add cells as needed, execute them and then continue to write other code that depends on the memory state generated by previous cells. You can in practice run cells in any order, which means in the process of experimentation you will have a machine state that was almost certainly not generated by the sequential execution of cells in the Notebook. This is perfectly illustrated by a recent study that found only 24 percent of open-source Jupyter Notebooks execute without errors.[7] The fix for the cell order problems, as observed by the authors, is to test code by restarting the kernel and executing from start to finish before committing Notebooks to your repository.

---

[5] Project Jupyter, https://jupyter.org/
[6] Apache Zeppelin, https://zeppelin.apache.org/
[7] J.F. Pimentel, L.G. Murta, V. Braganholo, and J. Freire. 2019. "A Large-Scale Study About Quality and Reproducibility of Jupyter Notebooks," *IEEE/ACM 16th International Conference on Mining Software Repositories (MSR)*, pp. 507–517.

The code reuse issue with Notebooks is that the way code is written does not encourage the creation of reusable functions. It is not easy to take a function written in a Notebook and refactor it into a library function that can be used in other experiments. Hence, without the ability or the incentive to do otherwise, users of Notebooks tend to write everything as long sections of procedural code that cannot be reused without large amounts of manual work. The only solution to this is to develop the internal discipline to create your own libraries and import them as needed. The tool itself, unfortunately does not help.

The final problem with Notebooks is code deployment. There have been attempts to build production systems that use Notebook-based code as the deployable artifact. Thankfully this approach seems to be in retreat, due to the previous two reasons, combined with the fact that the code is typically poorly written, unoptimized, full of superfluous sections, and engineers do not want to be responsible for maintaining bloated Notebook code artifacts.

The solution to this problem is again discipline. You should ensure that the code base for your deployable objects is maintained outside of the Notebook. The Notebook itself can be used for training, experimentation, and visualization. Any trained models should be exported as binary objects that can be imported into a production system. This approach gives you the rapid experimentation advantages of Notebooks but enforces the maintenance of production-ready codebases.

Data Management

The tools built in data science projects, not surprisingly, depend heavily on data. This dependency means that the repeatability and testing of experiments and solutions also depend on data. Data is typically not handled well by using source control, README files, or Notebooks. Data sets are typically too large to fit in source control, and even when they do it would break common practices of code separation. Data sets are also likely to be updated with some regularity, which means that producing repeatable results can be undermined by the data itself.

Good data science project management demands a solution to this problem. Solutions typically depend on the nature of the data and the underlying systems. In the simplest of situations data is extracted from a data warehouse and the updates guaranteed to only ever perform addition of new records. This permits you to include timestamp-based extraction scripts in your experiments that deliberately build temporary data sets as needed.

At the other extreme you might have raw data captured in streams that are processed by multiple systems, or a data warehouse that is continually overwritten as records are updated. In these situations, it is worthwhile creating a development (DEV) environment that contains a snapshot of the data sources at a point in time. This data can be used for realistic experimentation, as it is real data captured at a specific point in history. You will likely want multiple historical snapshots so that you can test the effects of data change over time. Ideally, these snapshots would have been created on a regular cadence with some underlying business imperative.

The DEV environment and its collection of data snapshots is potentially quite large and creates a weak spot in the reproducibility of your work. But it may be unavoidable. The snapshot should be created as an immutable reference data set against which an experiment runs. You may be able to store them in object storage and reinstantiate them as they are needed. Each experiment you write can, in principle, contain code to reinstantiate the data set, making it transparent which snapshot was used. Additional tests can then be written that simply change the snapshot to evaluate on more recent or older data.

With these principles in place, you will have devised a methodology that permits you to revisit the history of your own work, and others on your team. Any one in your team can repeat, modify, or correct any of the previous experiments.

Customer Check-In

Despite how well you feel you know what needs to done to complete a project, you should always have regular check-in sessions with a client to ensure alignment. There is always a danger that there has been a miscommunication between yourself and the client in the scoping phase. In the early stages of a project, the client can experience discussion fatigue and impatience to get to the building stage. For these reasons, they may have skipped some details or agreed to what you suggested simply to move forward.

In addition, it can be difficult for a client to understand how much work is involved moving from a concept to a reality. Software engineers face this dilemma all the time; once a client sees a mock-up, they feel that the product is mostly built. Even when they know intellectually that the work is not done, they still behave as if it should be already halfway complete.

Regular check-ins with your client can alleviate these problems. It will keep them abreast of progress and make them privy to obstacles as they occur. It will give them insight into the process and can potentially help them identify shortcuts that can be taken. For example, it is often the case that the list of requirements and features we have derived in the early stages of the engagement are not all equal in importance. If a client sees that you are experiencing difficulty satisfying all the requirements for building one particular piece of functionality, they may be prepared to sacrifice it for the sake of keeping a project on track and under budget. Such features can be shunted into the future work pile.

The check-in process also acts as a stopgap in case there has been a miscommunication. Every time you communicate results, show data and plots, you are forced to communicate your understanding of the problem. If you have misunderstood, the client is more likely to realize and point it out.

The regular check-in also gives the client an opportunity to change their mind, which can be a benefit or an impediment. This depends on the impetus for the change of mind. If the change is driven purely by them gaining an enhanced understanding of the problem space, then change is a good thing. You want them to recognize early on if they have set you toward solving the wrong problem. If, on the other hand, your client tends to be distracted by their latest ideas, and always chasing what they perceive as cutting edge, then you have a problem. In these situations, you will need to manage them, or manage the engagement; for example, you might need to meet with them slightly less regularly. Even so, you will need to make sure those check-in sessions contain enough new and exciting material that they remain enthused about the direction.

Check-ins are not always easy, and as I discussed above, they have the possibility to be an impediment to the success of a project. However, managed well, they can perform a crucial role of regulating your client's expectations and ensuring that the project is headed toward a successful outcome.

Deployment

Some data science projects will mature into a code base that becomes part of a production system. This is not true in all cases, and sometimes even if the intention is to modify a production system based on your work, you may not be involved in making those changes.

One of the reasons for this separation is that the interface between data science and software systems is not easy to manage. Even though data scientists can program, they typically have a very different approach to writing code that often does not mesh well with how software engineers like to produce and release code. The essence of the distinction is that data scientists usually want to produce ideas, insights, and results rapidly. They do not have to support their code and ensure it continues to run months or years after it was written. Software developers, on the other hand, have well-developed processes that are designed to ensure their code is written and released in ways that can be maintained and improved upon without causing major problems for an organization. There are a number of tools, both physical and social, that software engineers use to achieve these goals. Some of these processes are worth adopting for data science projects, while other aspects of data science work warrant new approaches.

We previously discussed the use of source control for managing code changes and repeatability. But software engineers do much more with source control. The approach varies, but there is one essential rule: any piece of code that will run on a production system must be first checked into a repository before it can be pushed into the production system. This rule ensures that there is an independent record of how every executable section of code came to be in the production system. There are a range of more complicated processes that are built on top of this essential idea. Most teams now use automated testing systems. In these systems, when code is checked into the production repository, automated tests run on it. The tests can detect things as trivial as whether the code conforms to style standards, all the way to testing individual functions against a variety of scenarios. The code is only able to be deployed into production if all tests are successful.

Another common process is what is called a "Pull Request" approach. In this approach, you are not able to check your code directly into the main branch of the production system. Instead, you must check it into a separate branch and then issue a "Pull Request" on that branch. This usually results in several lead developers being notified, who will then review the code before accepting it into the production system. This is essentially a formalized process around a code review that prevents code running in production without multiple people having agreed that it is ready. In your data science project these procedures may not need to be applied. However, you should be aware of and understand these ideas so that you are able to work with software developers.

In many instances, the cultural difference between data scientists and engineers is too significant for the teams to be working directly on the same code base. Either because of a lack of time or because of an insurmountable learning curve on either end. In these cases, you need to consider developing a methodology by which data scientists can contribute to a project through some limited subset of code, or through a scripting language.

The most inefficient solution that is sometimes chosen is that the software engineers rewrite the proposed solution using a language, framework, and methodology that is acceptable to their appetite for risk and support. If this approach is deemed necessary, then you should try and influence the way it is implemented. The worst possible outcome is when the production solution involves hard coding the original model, such that any change to the model requires software changes and compilation of the whole system. At a bare minimum it would be better to have the parameters of the model stored in a separate config file that can be updated more easily. Software engineers generally consider config changes to be easier to deploy than code changes.

A more productive solution is a design that will allow data scientists to contribute and update models on a regular basis. For example, a method by which data scientists can contribute configuration changes, serialized models, or scripts into the production framework. I have previously seen teams that restricted themselves to deploying linear models, and built production systems where models could be deployed, or modified, through a config file. The configuration described the model as a list of input features with their corresponding parameters, as well as an intercept and meta-parameters including a link function and the locations for loading data and storing results. In organizations that require large numbers of models, regularly updated, using standardized inputs, this can be a simple and effective way to deploy models.

The limiting impact of restricting deployment to linear models can be mitigated through well-planned feature engineering. In fact, there are numerous advantages to creating parallel independent processes for developing and releasing your data features regardless of how you are intending to deploy your work. Having a single well-tested code base that generates a wide range of metrics and fundamental business features will be useful, regardless of whether you are doing predictive modeling, building dashboards, or engaging in exploratory analysis. This is one of the design goals of a Feature Store, allowing you to manage the trade-off between model accuracy and management of production code. It will protect you against a proliferation of feature duplication where data scientists independently generate variations of the same features. Without a uniform definition of critical features, you can end up with confusion and greater potential for errors.

Decoupling the release of software components is a critical part of the modern software engineering. It allows software to be released with greater regularity and permits incremental improvements in the various decoupled components. You will likely discover that any organization you work for will be looking for ways to decouple the components of any solution. In data science this could include automated model retraining, intervention selection, optimization, and monitoring. You can prepare for these future requirements by actively looking for opportunities to decouple what you build. Identify any aspect of your system that can be separated so that it can be released and modified independently. Build these individual components in such a way that interoperation relies only on a well defined interface between them. Internal details of the implementation should be irrelevant to other parts of the system.

Summary

This chapter covered several key ideas that will help you deliver reliable work that can be integrated into your client's organization. You should continue to have regular check-in meetings with your client throughout the delivery period, the time cost these impose is worth the reduction in risk of the project not meeting expectations.

There are a variety of software and project management ideas you would be well served to adopt. You will want to use source control and documentation to improve the quality and reproducibility of your work. You need to be aware of the limitations of using Notebooks and some of the core considerations that software engineers have in mind when they think about production-ready code. Finally, you should be thinking about how your work can be separated into independent decoupled components that will make deployment and maintenance of your solution easier and durable for the long term.

CHAPTER 18

Estimating ROI

For most organizations, you will not be able to deploy a model until you have an estimate of the potential ROI of using the model. This ROI should be calculated as a tangible dollar impact over a prescribed period. Any potentially intangible effects, like customer experience or brand value, should be converted to nominal tangible values. In the vast majority of instances, intangible benefits are only beneficial because they ultimately have tangible impact, regardless of how difficult it is to measure them.

To do this well, you will need to analyze the way your work will impact individual elements of the business process. Looking at what will change and how that leads to specific financial returns. This process demands thinking about the potential for impacts outside of the immediate business problem. Cannibalization effects are one such difficult problem; success with a new process or product can result in reduced sales within another part of the business. For example, McDonalds took time to realize that when they promoted fish fillets, they sold fewer Quarter Pounders.[1]

Groundwork

When we have reached this stage of the project, we should have laid considerable groundwork for an ROI estimate. We worked with our client to collect information about the business context of the problem, derived metrics to measure the problem, and agreed upon a success metric for the project. We have worked through the constraints that operate on any potential solution that will help understand the economic feasibility of anything that might be proposed.

---

[1] D. McCann. 2014. "Predictive Analytics: How Clear Is the ROI?," *CFO Magazine.* www.cfo.com/technology/2014/07/predictive-analytics-clear-roi/

All the discussion up to this point will have provided the fundamental atoms of information that go into an ROI estimate: How many events or rows of data do we need to process in a given period of time? What are the possible actions we could take? What are the estimates of the financial impact of all possible outcomes? For predictive modeling projects, we discussed the way that the cost/benefit considerations can be utilized in the choice of model and its optimization.

If the information described in the previous paragraph is absent from your project documents, then I encourage you to return to the earlier chapters and use them to help obtain the required context. There are many reasons why you may be reading this chapter without that information. Perhaps, you were deep into the project before buying this book, or perhaps you have been handed someone else's project. Regardless of how you arrived here, to move forward you will need to make a business case for your solution, which means gaining an understanding the fundamentals of the business process and the expected impact of changing it.

Estimate or Measure

There are multiple common points of confusion in industry about what it means to estimate ROI. Some people believe that ROI estimation and measurement are virtually synonymous. This is because they are of the opinion that the only way to estimate the ROI of a larger project is to run a small pilot program in which you directly measure ROI and extrapolate that return to the larger population.

This measure and extrapolate is a valid approach, but by no means the only approach. Moreover, most pilot programs are also not without costs, so an organization would be well advised to do some form of ROI estimate even before running a pilot. A model that appears very unlikely to have an ROI is not worth putting into a pilot program.

How can we estimate ROI without a pilot program?

The key to answering that question is understanding how the solution we are deploying will be used. What are the decisions that will be made or the processes that will change? It involves laying out the expected relative costs and benefits of all possible outcomes of those decisions and processes. It involves recognizing that being able to identify, predict, or alert on something does not guarantee you can change it. Hence, you need to estimate the probability of being able to effect that change. Ideally, we also quantify our uncertainty about all the potential outcomes, so that we can provide bounds on our ROI estimates.

For our ROI estimates to be informative, it is essential that we understand the true performance of the model. This means that any metrics of performance have been produced in an unbiased way; in other words, using representative out-of-sample data, such that we can reasonably expect the model will perform similarly in the future. If these estimates are overconfident, then so will our ROI estimate and the success of the project is threatened.[2]

Model to Outcome

The difficulty of generating robust detail-oriented ROI estimates depends very much on the type of problem you are solving. It could be as simple as estimating the impact of a single change to an automated decision-making process. In other instances, it will involve considering how an entire business process could be reorganized and simulating the expected outcome.

Regardless of the complexity, you are always estimating the impact of a change in business outcomes, resulting from changes that almost certainly involve decision making. There are many fine details about how a business operates that need to be considered when performing these estimations. However, there are a number of general patterns that tend to occur repeatedly. For the purposes of discussion, I have put these patterns into the following categories:

1. Discrete Decisions
    1.1 Decision with deterministic outcomes
    1.2 Decisions with stochastic outcomes
2. Continuous Responses
    2.1 Individual Impacts
    2.2 Aggregated Impacts

---

[2] R. Pahuja. 2021. "Is This the Reason Your ML Model Is Failing to Deliver ROI?," *ETCIO*. https://cio.economictimes.indiatimes.com

3. Reorganization
    3.1 Optimization
    3.2 Strategic Insight

These general categories cover the majority of applications of data science to business. In the first top-level category, you are running your model to help the business make some kind decision between a finite set of options (do X or do Y). Often the data science solution is itself generating this binary outcome, but not always.

In the second top-level category, your solution produces some numerical value, which the business includes such that the magnitude of the quantity is materially important in the decision. In other words, the value produced by your solution exerts material influence on some business process, for example, the expected number of days until some machinery will require service is used to schedule maintenance.

You may observe that these first two categories map perfectly to the machine learning categories of classification and regression. This is not guaranteed to be the case. Many uses of classification models involve directly using the output probability (a numerical quantity), and many instances of regression ultimately drive simple binary decisions. In addition, organizations can use analytics or unsupervised models to drive all kinds of decisions. It may be true that in many of these instances there would be an improved framing of the machine learning approach that would better suit the desired outcome. But that does not change the fact that people can and do use these techniques in ways that do not map perfectly to the categories of action.

The third top-level category of business impact refers to situations in which you want to use a model to reorganize some part of the business operations—typically this will be to optimize toward some goal. But sometimes there are more general strategic changes that are made with insufficient information to really call it optimization. The difference with the preceding two categories is that the model is applied in a global fashion to restructure something, rather than being used operationally to deal with events on a case-by-case basis. The goal of estimating the ROI in this third category is to determine whether certain global changes could improve overall outcomes.

Within these broad categories there are a number of natural ways to create subcategories. The subcategories I have chosen here are those that I have seen most frequently in one form or another. More complex situations tend to involve some combination of many of these elements, something that you will need to extract by understanding the business. Nevertheless, I find this hierarchy and classification very useful in quickly focusing a discussion on what is needed to get a sense of how to estimate the impact of a model. To this end, we shall explore each of these scenarios more deeply.

Discrete Decisions Deterministic Outcomes

Discrete decisions involve choices between a finite set of options. They are made with the underlying assumption that doing so will result in a beneficial outcome. In certain scenarios, the outcome of the action could be deterministic; for example, if you reject a transaction because it appears fraudulent, then the transaction is denied. Because the transaction processing is under your control then the action produces a deterministic result. The transaction does not happen, and your fee is not earned. Now the transaction was either generated by a customer or a criminal, so either a customer is annoyed with you, or you have prevented an instance of fraud. However, your rigorous backtesting of the model will tell you about the relative rates at which these events are expected to occur. Hence, if you can assign costs and benefits to all possible outcomes for the fraud and nonfraud scenarios, you can extrapolate from the number of cases you expect to see over a given time and directly estimate the impact.

This specific scenario is the one you see most often when people demonstrate ROI for machine learning using a cost matrix. The details of this calculation are as follows: For each potential threshold of the model, you use your validation or holdout data to calculate the expected rate of true positives, false positives, true negatives, and false negatives. You then apply these rates to the expected number of cases you will see over the period of time you want to do the ROI estimate. For example, you might be processing ten thousand transactions per month, of which approximately one hundred turn out to be fraudulent. Now, if you start with a threshold at which the true positive rate is 0.3 and the false positive rate is 0.01, that means you will catch 30 percent of the true fraud (30 cases) and you will mistakenly identify 1 percent of the nonfraud as fraud (99 cases). You must also be missing 70 percent of the true fraud (the false negatives) and correctly identifying 99 percent of the true nonfraud (the true negatives).

You should be able to put a dollar value on each of these outcomes. Typically, catching the true positives is the goal and will have the largest impact. In this case, let's say $5,000 benefit per case on average. However, the false positives also have an impact (canceling genuine transactions means lost revenue and irritating customers), let's say $500 on average. So, on this ledger the benefit is $5,000 \times 30 - 99 \times 500 = \$100,500$

Alternatively, you could assign a cost to all the fraudulent transactions you are missing, this is money lost every time one of the instances of fraud transpires. Typically, this cost is already being incurred by the business so it should probably be left out of an ROI estimation, because the status quo is the baseline against which you are trying to improve. The exception to this is when you are benchmarking against the ROI of an existing model. In which case you need to either estimate the cost/benefit of both against the same baseline, or add conditional logic to the evaluation of the new model so that it only penalizes the model when it makes mistakes that the previous model did not.

You should be careful not to double count when assigning these costs and benefits. Each cost/benefit should only be attached to a single side of the ledger: there is either a cost to missing fraud or a benefit to catching it. Which side you place the cost/benefit on depends on the baseline you are measuring against. If we included the $5,000 on both sides in our example, then we are biasing the ROI estimation toward the true positive/ false negative trade-off, reducing the impact of the false positives. In other words, our ROI estimate would be an overestimate that downplayed the true cost of annoying our customer base.

An alternative approach to assigning the costs and benefits is to break the impact of your true positives and false negatives into multiple components. In this example, you could associate the direct financial impact with one side of the equation. For example, the benefit of catching the fraud is associated with the true positives. On the other side, you can include an estimate of the reputation or brand damage by not catching the fraud. This approach is particularly useful if you expect asymmetry in the cost benefit: you might argue that people notice more when fraud has been committed against them than when you have caught it. Hence there is a larger brand cost to not catching fraud than the brand impact of catching it. If you choose to take a more detailed approach to assigning costs and benefits, just be sure to be aware of each of the individual cost/benefit components and ensure that each of these individual components are only counted on one side of the ledger.

If you analyze a model at a given output threshold, you will have an estimate of the number of cases that will fall into each of these different buckets. If you combine these estimates with the estimated costs/benefits of all outcomes, you can estimate the overall ROI impact of using the model for that decision at that threshold.

In principle, you can iterate over all potential thresholds in the output of a model and repeat the above process. By considering the expected outcomes at each of these thresholds you can then estimate the overall ROI (or loss) at each threshold and optimize, choosing the threshold that gives the best return. Ultimately your estimate of the best possible return using a given model determines whether the model is worth deploying.

The approach outlined above, of discrete decisions with deterministic outcomes, can easily scale when you have multiple decisions to make. These decisions could be driven by taking several different thresholds and making a decision based on where the score sits. It could be driven by some hierarchy of models, or a multiclass classifier. The key is that in each case there are a discrete number of options. The option you choose is based on one or more models, and the outcomes of those decisions can be calculated directly because the outcome is deterministic.

Discrete Decisions Stochastic Outcomes

Sometimes when you make a decision based on a model output, you will be taking an action whose intended outcome is not guaranteed. For example, you may be predicting customer churn and you want to prevent it. There is no way to ensure the action you take will effectively prevent a customer from closing their account. Hence, we say the outcome is stochastic, the result of our intervention is itself a random variable.

We can estimate the likelihood of success of an action, either by simple estimation from previous attempts or by modeling it. For example, if you have sent an e-mail with a discount or special offer to your customers previously, then you will know what the uptake rate of the offer was; this forms an estimate of the success rate of that intervention. Alternatively, you could build a second model that will predict the likelihood of intervention success from customer attributes using historical data on the same intervention.

Once you have a method of estimating the probability that your intervention will work, you can return to estimate the ROI. Much like the first scenario we discussed, you are evaluating multiple potential model thresholds, looking at the number of actions that would need to be taken, the cost of the action, the probability of success, and the estimated benefit in those instances where it does work versus the costs when it fails.

It should be clear to you that the first scenario we discussed, concerning deterministic outcomes, is a special case of the indeterministic outcomes class. It is the scenario in which the probability of intervention success is equal to one. Similar to the way we did in the deterministic case, we can extrapolate the scenario to think about taking multiple different actions or choosing from multiple options where, in each case, we require an estimate of the probability of success. Some of those actions could be deterministic, meaning that we are estimating ROI over a mixture of stochastic and deterministic interventions. The cost matrix could be high dimensional and complicated, but it will be finite and estimable.

Continuous Responses Individual Impact

In the situation where our action space is continuous, we are not taking discrete actions. Instead, we are taking actions that have a real valued quantitative component. This could be choosing a price, discount, or quantity to stock. Typically, the numerical value returned by our model is used in the business process to determine the required quantity.

Genuine continuous responses can be sometimes difficult to identify. Just because a model produces a continuous value (expected sale price of a car or expected time until an employee quits) does not mean that the business has a continuous response. As we have discussed previously, a business can often apply thresholds to the output of such models for binary decisions.

True continuous responses tend to occur where the business process uses a real value in the action itself. For example, the amount to bid on an ad-unit for an automated marketing process, or the discount rate to offer a customer based on their conversion propensity and expected value. In both instances, you may be tasked with predicting that output directly, but you may also be providing a model that predicts something that feeds into the mathematical logic that decides on these bid prices or discount rates.

In both examples, we can estimate the ROI of each individual prediction. In the second example, we might have a model that predicts the conversion propensity from a proposed discount level. If we presume that the probabilities produced by that model are well calibrated, then the estimated ROI of the discount model is the difference between the base conversion rate multiplied by the lifetime value of the customer, and the discount model conversion rate multiplied by the discounted lifetime value.

In this example, the model selection process would likely scan across potential discounts and choose the one that maximizes return (subject to other business conditions). In many instances, you might expect that no discount is chosen because the customer is not sufficiently price sensitive. However, the critical thing to note is that the process produces a continuous output, and that the total expected ROI can be estimated as a summation over a sample of individual historical (or simulated) records. In other words, the contribution of each model output to ROI is independent.

Continuous Responses Aggregated Impact

In some continuous response cases, it is not possible to estimate ROI at the level of the individual predictions. This is because the decision making, or business action, does not occur at the level of individual events.

You can find many examples of this in media and marketing use cases. Models that forecast the number of people who will be watching a given television program are used to influence the purchase of advertising inventory. Television stations want to maximize the revenue generated from selling advertising on these ad-slots. However, the ad-slots are not generally sold individually, they are sold in blocks for a campaign that covers multiple ad-slots. The televisions station only makes guarantees about the estimated number of people who would see the entire campaign. This means that what matters for ROI estimation is the expected aggregate error over a campaign, not the error made on the individual slots.

You may well think to yourself, as long as the error over all the slots has a mean of zero this problem should take care of itself. An unbiased estimator will balance out the over- and underpredictions, so that the aggregate will be very minimal. This is what I thought when I first encountered this problem. What makes this scenario problematic is that the blocks of advertising sold for a campaign are not randomly selected. Ad campaigns fall into a number of potential groupings determined by the product type and the desired audience. The different advertisers and brands will all have preferences in the inventory they run on. The consequence of these complications means you need to try and ensure a model has zero mean error across an open-ended collection of nonrandom subsets of the inventory.

I have encountered similar problems dealing with forecasting and optimizing other aspects of digital advertising. If we abstract away from all the specifics, the core problem is that the relationship between forecast errors and ROI can only be calculated across multiple aggregations of the forecasts. Furthermore, the specific aggregations used by the business operations are not predetermined and form a partially stochastic decision process.

How can we estimate the ROI in such a situation?

The approach you can take depends on the structure of the process. What kind of time period do you need to aggregate over, how many different combinations are important and how random is the selection of combinations? Can you identify levels for which the expected number of combinations is approximately deterministic?

For example, if in the case of ad-slots, we discover that certain groups of ad-slots are routinely sold together in a block, then we can evaluate error on these common groupings. This might be morning TV and after-school TV, or slots between 7 and 10 p.m. Any common grouping provides an adequate set of groups to evaluate independently. Evaluate the estimated ROI on each aggregation and sum them up for an overall estimate of ROI.

In other situations, you may find that the number of potential combinations is too large, or randomness plays too strong a role to be able to define the required groups. A common indicator of this situation is that the business stakeholders will struggle to describe what constitutes the expected set of combinations over any given period. If they share the operational business data, you may find no such reliable pattern that you could exploit.

What to do in this face of such complexity?

The core problem at the source of this conundrum is that we need to estimate the ROI of a model when the business cannot give us deterministic rules that define the impact of a model output on a decision or action. There are a number of approaches to this that can be used independently or in tandem. First, you can perform ROI backtests where you collect additional data about the financial deals that have been done over a period that corresponds to a backtest data set of the model. For example, we might have six months of advertising campaigns that were sold over a period of time, along with the exact ad-slots that were included in each deal. We apply our model, predict audience numbers, and then identify which of those deals we successfully identified as over- or underperforming. Each of these situations will require an estimate of cost or benefit. In this example it would be the value of wasted inventory, or the ability to make use of inventory that was overprovided and undercapitalized.

The business backtest has the advantage of communicating the potential value to the business in terms of real deals they will be familiar with. Your stakeholders should already have intimate knowledge of what has transpired over the last 6 to 12 months, and seeing that recent history pulled apart and transformed into an alternative set of outcomes makes for a convincing argument. However, it does not necessarily communicate how the model or system will perform moving forward in time.

An alternative approach that allows you to investigate model performance under potential future scenarios is simulation. We discussed simulation in a previous chapter when discussing the development of your models. Simulation of the business context and decision-making process allows you to investigate how the model performs under conditions that you control. Simulation is not without its difficulties; you will need to explicate all (or a sufficient subset) of the relevant variables in the business context and then estimate the distributions and dependencies between these variables. This information will need to come from a combination of deep Q&A processes and examination of operational data.

A common simulation process is to sample from the distributions collected from historical data to generate outcomes that will occur at frequencies representative of the real-world outcomes. For each generated outcome you calculate the expected return. You will then have a probability distribution over ROI. You can provide an estimate as a confidence bounds on the ROI.

Collecting these parameters and estimating them will be difficult and time consuming. Although it comes with the advantage of providing detailed insight into how your model will interact with the real-world process. You can test upper and lower bounds on outcomes through repeated simulation, and even provide probability estimates of the likelihood of certain outcomes by treating the entire process as a Monte Carlo simulation.

Perhaps the greatest difficulty of this approach is convincing business-people that it is informative. Regardless of how well entrenched Monte Carlo simulations are in the physical sciences, the word simulation does not seem to engender trust from business stakeholders. To mitigate these difficulties, I have two suggestions. The first is to have a concise explanation of what the simulation does. Emphasize that the fundamental variables and probabilities have been drawn from their own data and insights. Secondly, have a story about why chance plays a role in the actual business outcomes. I quite often rely on sporting analogies, referring to the fact that even the best team is not guaranteed to win every game. You are trying to help the business understand that they need to model the expected number of times that a model will drive a beneficial outcome in a given period of time, without making guarantees.

Optimization and Business Reorganization

Not all work you do will be used operationally at the level of individual decisions. Sometimes analysis or models are inputs that feed into a high-level reorganization of the business process itself. In this case, the goal is to change how that business process functions to achieve a permanent impact on some outcome: to increase the throughput, reduce the errors, reduce costs, and so on.

Canonical optimization projects allow you to apply predetermined patterns of constraints onto an algebraic expression of the business process. Unfortunately, these situations represent a fraction of all the real-world processes that a business would like to optimize. Note, I am using the term optimize here in its common sense. The word optimization predates its usage in academia and is commonly used in business to simply mean improve or move toward optimal.

We have previously discussed many of the complications of optimizing processes that are not explicitly defined and require varying degrees of modeling and simulation. You can easily find yourself working on projects that are not explicitly defined as optimization, but as the final impact on the business is a restructuring of the process, then it is an optimization in some sense.

The fundamental goal of the ROI estimate is to generate a reasonable estimate of expected return. Be explicit with assumptions, quantify the uncertainties, and calculate return over these uncertainties. If the optimization process itself involves simulation, then the simulated outcomes serve as a source for ROI estimates under different conditions.

Critical to any expectation calculation is well-calibrated probabilities. Regardless of whether they are parameters estimated by the business, or the outputs of models, you should verify the probabilities used in your estimate. Ideally, run calculations on different estimates to evaluate the sensitivity of the ROI to each of the components in your approach.

Strategic Insight

The final category of model to value we have is something of a catch-all. When your work is not going to be integrated directly into a business process of any kind, either operationally or through reorganization, then it is likely the intended purpose is strategic.

If your strategic insights project is going to generate real value, then you will have been working with your sponsor to develop a set of candidate insights, recommendations, and actions throughout the course of the project. Each iteration of exploration and modeling will have been steered in a direction in which your sponsor sees value. If your sponsor is pragmatic, then this value should have begun to have been articulated as a set of decisions that hinge on the accuracy of your insights. Your sponsor should be seeing estimable value in the consequences of those decisions.

It is recommended that during this process you ask for quantification of that impact. Many sponsors will be reluctant to give specific dollar values, in which case you can ask for general indication of the source of value or proportional quantification. For example:

"How much could this improve the product?"
"Will there be cost savings in changing location?"
"What is your estimate of the size of the market?"

It is quite likely that while talking at a high level, your sponsor will reveal some of the internal calculations they are using to determine relative value. These may be some very rough back-of-the-envelope calculations. But if you gain some insight into them, you will be able to judge how robust they are and encourage your sponsor to firm them up or make them more realistic. Ideally, you will get to a point where you and your sponsor feel comfortable with the estimates and the sponsor feels they have not had to reveal business critical information.

Summary

Estimating project ROI can be difficult for multiple reasons, the connection between the data science work and the business impact may not be direct, and your sponsor may be reluctant to talk about the financial details of their organization. In this chapter, we discussed multiple general categories of how data science work interfaces with processes and decisions. Identifying where your project lies on the spectrum quickly, will help in gathering the information you need to start estimating the project's potential impact, and ultimately make a compelling business case for deployment.

A strong business case typically requires a detailed analysis of how your project exerts material impact on the business. This allows you to understand the financial impact on individual events in the business and scale those up to estimate the impact on the total business unit over an extended period of time.

CHAPTER 19

Deployment

Deploying models into production systems is not always part of the data scientist's work process. Many data science projects are not explicitly undertaken to build production systems, and even among those that are, the data science results are generally handed to an engineering team for the final implementation. However, there are often data science specific requirement to the deployment process. So, to achieve effective outcomes, it is worthwhile for data scientists to have some involvement in the deployment process.

In the preceding chapters, we have discussed many kinds of data science projects and the interface they have with business operations. There is a weak sense in which any project that achieves an impact has been deployed. To be impactful, change needs to happen and the change can be considered a form of deployment. For example, if your analysis results in a redesign of a product or service, then this is a form of deployment. Whenever something changes based on the modeling you have done, then you have created a production solution.

One of the most satisfying outcomes for a data scientist is getting a model delivered in such a way that an automated decision is used to improve a business process. This is the form of deployment that we will focus on in this chapter, because it is the sense in which the term deployment is most commonly used. Unfortunately, getting models deployed into production in this way is hard. It is so hard, that industry surveys consistently suggest organizations have persistent problems getting models into production.[1]

Many of the problems of deployment are related to data science teams not taking the production system into consideration during the

---

[1] T. Davenport, and K. Malone. 2021. "Deployment as a Critical Business Data Science Discipline," *Harvard Data Science Review*. https://doi.org/10.1162/99608f92.90814c32

development phase. In a previous chapter, we explored the importance of thinking about timing, data availability, and technology stack when delivering your data science solution. In this chapter, we are going to focus on additional project management topics and strategies for effective deployment.

The Handover

The most common interface between a data science team and the engineering team that maintains a production system will be a software artifact. This could be a serialized model, it could be a JSON or XML depiction of the required parameters, or it could be a script or application to be deployed. A common problem with deployment is that the engineering team are not happy with the quality of the artifact, or unhappy about the format and technology it uses. The best antidote to this situation is early discussion. If the engineering team have some experience in the deployment of data science, you will likely be told what format to use. It will be up to you to understand the limitations of that format as soon as possible. Determine if an adequate solution can be delivered that way and begin negotiating for change if not.

If the engineering team has no experience with deployment of data science solutions, then you may be asked for some recommendations. Do not be too quick to recommend your favorite technology. You should take the time to understand their existing tech stack and think about what supporting new technologies would involve. Understanding the technology stack involves asking for an architecture diagram that depicts major system components and how they interface. You should ask about the organizations appetite for custom code versus off-the-shelf systems. You should ask which programming languages the engineering teams are experienced in and are currently supporting. You should ask about the application design principles they tend to use, and which technologies and approaches are being phased out.

If the line of questioning outlined in the previous paragraph is alien to you, then I suggest you find an ally or mentor with engineering experience. Ideally, they would be someone inside the organization you are working with. That way you can talk about the requirements of the data science solution being built and learn from them about the kinds of system constraints in the existing system architecture.

Try to find a recommendation that balances the needs of an effective data science solution, and one that is maintainable for the organization. In the extreme case, when a completely new tech stack is required, you will need to be transparent about this. Your stakeholders will need to build a business case that the benefits of the solution justify not just your payment, but the ongoing maintenance costs of the technologies it requires.

IT Departments

For many organizations your biggest challenge to getting models in production is going to be the IT department. IT departments carry a lot of weight in larger organizations because of the extent to which businesses depend on them for many critical services. The importance of modern IT departments has made them naturally conservative in nature.

An IT department will generally resist any proposed change regardless of how trivial it is. This is because they are painfully aware of how easily mistakes can creep in, and how costly they are to find and repair. If the proposed change involves new systems, then the resistance will be stronger, simply because new systems mean new support loads for IT. These forms of resistance are normal, and what should be expected given the nature and gravity of what IT must deliver.

To overcome their resistance, you will need to learn their language, build very strong business cases, and have strategies for mitigating their concerns. For example, you need to be clear about where the support burden for your models resides. Ideally, IT will be responsible for the generic hardware and software systems that your models run on. This induces a minor support burden, but one that is expected with business growth. It does not involve new skill sets, merely supporting new servers of the same form.

This strategy does mean that you need to think about who in your team will be responsible for monitoring and maintaining models. If you are consulting to another company, you will need to communicate to your stakeholders that they will need support staff who can take on the role of supporting the data science products.

If you are in the situation of working with a client to outline what the support model looks like, you should also be thinking about failure conditions. What does the business process do if the model fails to return a result? What if the monitoring process detects that performance of the model has deteriorated? A solid baseline solution to this problem is failover to status quo. In other words, when the new system fails, hard code a default that returns to the historical behavior. In many instances you want to ensure that the worst possible outcome is what is currently happening.

Data Science Is Not IT

You may encounter some very specific organizational problems when dealing with IT departments. The source of this will be people in IT who believe that data science should be conducted and governed within IT. As data science involves writing programs and delivering software solutions of a certain kind, some IT professionals believe that it should be subject to all the standard processes of IT.

This political issue is difficult to navigate, in part because these IT people can be mistaken about how well they understand statistics and machine learning. They will want to bring the data science project into their agile processes, with software specifications, stand-ups, quality assurance testing (QAT), user acceptance testing (UAT), and so on. Which is not to say that any of these is individually bad. But it can be difficult to explain that the work you are doing in a sprint cannot be predefined, because it will depend on the results of the first experiment.

The core reason that data science does not fit into these processes is because software engineering (in corporate IT) is typically not experimentation led, it is focused on delivering features. They have clients who give them requirements, they negotiate until the requirements are realistic, then they prioritize and build. Almost everything is decided in advance of it being done, it is planned out, then implemented and delivered. Of critical importance is that software engineers are encouraged to break down the large goals into smaller concrete tasks that they can deliver in estimable chunks of time, so that the entire process of delivering a changing software product can be managed.

Data science typically does not proceed toward the predictable building of a large collection of predefined goals. At the most macroscopic and trivial level you could state the goals of a data science project. However, data scientists are typically trying and discarding many approaches based on experimentation and changing their direction as they proceed. Conforming to IT processes in the way software developers do would mean wasting enormous amounts of time specifying and breaking down tasks that end up being discarded.

In general, the best approach you can use when pushed to adhere to these practices, is to compromise by adopting them at a high level so that your role in the overall delivery is clear. For example, by submitting high-level goals or deliverables as tasks for the scrum board. At the same time explaining why the individual steps required are fluid and depend on the results of experiments. By participating in the overall process, you allow the managers involved to understand where your work fits, and you can then educate them on what makes data science unique.

Once you have solved the political and cultural problems of integrating your work with operations and IT, you need to work with them on solving a range of problems together. You will need to solve the logistics of generating and managing the required data, at the required time, and ensuring the results are made available to the systems that need to act. In addition to these fundamental questions about integrating your model, there are a range of broader system architecture decisions that you may be asked to participate in.

Systems Architecture

There are a range of considerations for a model deployment architecture that engineers will be concerned with. The primary concern will be the expected throughput of records to process and the speed with which they need to be processed. The processing time will include all data collection, aggregation, and preparation as well as any model outputs that need to be generated. The speed of processing will be subject to the latency requirements of the system. These considerations will be different for systems that process individual customer requests in real time (e.g., predicting potential account takeover events as customers use a system), versus batch processes that occur on a schedule (e.g., processing all customers to update a predicted likelihood of churn). There will be latency requirements in both situations, but usually the requirements of the former are more stringent than the latter.

Engineering teams will also be concerned with how errors are dealt with at each stage of the processing pipeline, and how they affect the system. For example, does an error on a single record prevent the entire process completing, or are all records completely independent. Are all stages completely dependent on the previous stage? Or can the system fall back to some default behavior or value under conditions of error. Finally, you will need to consider how the entire process will scale as the volumes of data and users increase over time. If you are operating in a small team or a low-budget project, then some of these considerations may fall to you. I suggest you find and befriend an architect or engineer with experience working with the systems you need to use. Your best approach will be to find someone with the experience that you can leverage.

There are a range of other deployment practices for prediction systems that engineers, and architects, will usually not have experience with. We will discuss these in the following section. As a data scientist you should develop a deep knowledge of these. Just like it was your job to make managers and businesspeople understand how a data science process works, when it comes to deployment it will be your job to communicate the unusual requirements of deploying models to engineering and operations staff.

Retraining and Redeployment

One of the less intuitive elements of production machine learning is understanding that models generally require regular replacement. What makes this unintuitive is the general sense that, for humans, once something is learned it is permanent. It is *like learning to ride a bike*, is a common expression that captures this sentiment.

You will need to explain to all stakeholders that models typically degrade in performance over time, which necessitates that pathways for retraining and redeploying models are built into the system design. You will be able to simulate the degradation through backtesting; however, you cannot anticipate large changes in the business context or operations that will drastically alter the performance of a model. For example, a new competitor entering a market, or a new technology can rapidly change the business landscape and render models invalid. Regardless of how stable a business appears, it is irresponsible to assume a model will not require an update.

One potential difficulty in designing a redeployment process, is determining the checks and balances that need to be passed. In software engineering there are a range of automated testing approaches that can be used, and these are well developed and applied across may organizations. Collectively, these tools and practices and often referred to as developer operations (DevOps).

Data science as a discipline has no standard approaches to this problem. As discussed in a previous chapter, DevOps practices can sometimes be applied to data science projects, but they typically do not test the most critical thing: performance on real data. In the absence of standards and best practices, there is only one principle you should rely on when designing your deployment process: identify the risks that are most critical to your client, and design tests to mitigate against those.

Automated Retraining

In many circumstances, an ideal state would be one in which the deployment environment not only detects problems but also includes automatic retraining and evaluation. Many, if not most, organizations are not ready to accept a process that allows a model into production that has not gone through some form of human review.

There is a trade-off between having an immutable model versus one that can automatically adapt. This is an architectural decision that can influence the business impact of your solution. Regular retraining is not always necessary, although some problems, like fraud detection, benefit so heavily from continuous retraining that it may be necessary from the start.

If you are going to recommend some form of automated retraining, you will need very strong evidence for the benefit it is going to provide. This will typically be a meta-level analysis: where you test not just whether a specific model delivers the results you want, but whether a process of continually retraining that model results in some improvement. To do this you need to run an experiment that simulates the continuous retraining process over a historical data set, and benchmark it against a static model trained on the data from the preceding period.

A general approach to running an experiment like this is as follows:

1. Collect data that spans a multiyear period.
2. Put aside the latest 12 months of data for the experiment.
3. Use the earlier data for your standard model building workflow.
4. Select a model based on performance on this previous time period.
5. Test that model on every month of data since that point (12 test results).
6. Start the retraining simulation.
7. Train two new models that are regularly retrained as we move forward in time:

    7.1 First model uses all data available prior to the test month.

    7.2 Second model uses a fixed window of data, taking the most recent data.

This process will generate performance metrics for three different modeling approaches on the 12 months of test data. If you plot the test performance of these models, over time, you will get a sense of the expected deterioration behavior of the original model. You can compare this with the two continuously retrained models. Of the two retrained models, you will also get an indication of whether there is any performance benefit or harm in using all the available data versus just training on more recent data.

You could run many versions of this experiment, varying the model being used and the length of the training window. However, the minimal version of the experiment will allow you to judge both the value of more recent data, and the expected model performance decay. These results allow you to illustrate to your stakeholders the cost/benefit trade-off in each retraining schedule.

If these experiments do not show significant deterioration of your models over time, there are other situations in which retraining will be desirable. The most common of these is that something in the underlying process of data changes fundamentally. These changes are not represented in the historical data, and hence the impact cannot be modeled, but it almost always necessitates retraining. For example, you roll out a new product or service that is fundamentally different from previous offerings. For this reason, it is worthwhile describing for your clients some of the hypothetical situations in which retraining will be desirable. Allow them to reflect on their business plans and determine how often and when retraining is going to be appropriate. You will need to be transparent about the costs of automated retraining, this could be as simple as the expected compute costs, or as complicated as the labor costs of a regular process of manual review and documentation preparation for regulators.

Feature Stores

One potential architectural feature of a large-scale data science system is a feature store. The idea of the feature store is a managed repository of data points used across multiple data science projects. The features are typically focused on business-specific analytical descriptors of the critical entities in your organization: customers, employees, products, locations, equipment, and so on. However, there are emerging conversations about including lower-level machine learning specific data into feature stores, such as representing embeddings and the data used to generate them inside feature stores.[2]

The features in the feature store should be modeling ready, meaning that effort has been made to ensure that anomalies in the source systems have already been resolved. The raw data has been examined, executive decisions about how to clean it have been made, and the data preparation has been implemented in a robust engineering-managed data processing pipeline that makes the features available. A key idea is that if you build models on the feature store, it contains data that is reflective of what the data will look like in the future: distributions, definitions, and so on.

The feature store can be used to deliver data to production systems, as well as being continuously expanded as needed. When you add new data sources and features, they are first deployed into the feature store. Experiments can then be conducted; promising candidates can then be moved to evaluation in preprod stages. When a model finally makes it

---

[2] L.. Orr, A. Sanyal, X. Ling, K. Goel, and M. Leszczynski. 2021. "Managing ML Pipelines: Feature Stores and the Coming Wave of Embedding Ecosystems," *Preprint*. https://arxiv.org/abs/2108.05053

into production, the features that it needs will be already available and up to date in the production feature store.

There are multiple challenges in building robust feature stores. Models can require data that has different latencies and requires different levels of aggregation. For example, some models might involve real-time scoring of customers immediately as they log into a website, in which case the features used are derived from the context of their login and their immediate behavior on the website. Other models might involve monthly scoring in a batch job that requires many time-consuming aggregation jobs to be run over their transaction history.

In an ideal feature store, the features would be broken into groups of data points that are combined into sets based on a combination of the entities they represent, the source systems, and the latency of their calculation. For example, your customer data set might consist of a base table containing demographics and account details. For the web login scenario described in the previous paragraph, the customer base data may be joined with a feature set summarizing their previous and current login sessions. For the batch scoring job, the web behavior might be ignored; instead, you join the customer base data with a set of transactional aggregation features that are generated monthly as a prerequisite for the batch scoring job.

The feature store, with its internal structure, becomes a reusable resource that can benefit your entire data science team. In fact, if there was one single way that you could maximize reuse and reduce the loss of IP in your data science team, it would be getting more data science work captured in a feature store. The reason is that many features developed for one specific project can end up delivering value for other projects. Data scientists can quickly set up experiments to scour the feature store for data points that will help them with new problems.

The most significant downside to a feature store architecture approach is that it creates coupling between components of your data science stack. Models that would be otherwise independent now depend on a single resource. This makes changes and updates increasingly difficult. Consequently, the feature store can be an impediment to agility and innovation. An ideal data science stack would contain robust versioning of features in a feature store, permitting flexibility in how the system evolves, and allow data science teams to deploy thoroughly independent models where it is appropriate.

Preparation for Stacking

One of the most fruitful themes in the development of machine learning has been the variety of approaches to combining multiple models into an ensemble. Some ensemble techniques will be specific to each project you are working on. They contain processes internal to the learning algorithm that create the ensemble for the specific problem.

Stacking is an ensemble technique in which completely independent models are combined by training a final model on the outputs of all the underlying models. You can include some or all the original features in the input for the final model. The core idea is that the final model learns the strengths and weaknesses of the underlying models and produces a superior output.

One way of designing a production system to exploit this approach to modeling is to push the results of each of your models into a section of the feature store so that they are available for building new models in the future. The primary difficulty of doing this well is controlling for overfitting and target leakage. The problem is that the model outputs might be generated by models that have been exposed to the signals we are trying to predict.

To solve these problems, you need to ensure that any model outputs you record in the feature store are all out of sample. Initial results could be from cross validation, but because of the pernicious nature of time sensitivity in many problems you are generally better off doing out-of-time scoring of the data.

Storing out-of-sample scores within the feature store is useful for more than just potential ensembles. It also allows for easy discovery, and potentially automation, of reusable code. By exploring previous model outputs as features, you can discover if any previous data science projects across your organization are using approaches that could deliver value for your own project.

Summary

Deploying data science solutions requires solving a range of problems that are new for most organizations. Effective solutions demand data scientists that think about the requirements of the production environment. Deployed solutions will inevitably need replacement and may even require an automated process of retraining or adjustment.

There are several data science production architecture decisions that you may be involved in. Feature stores allow organizations to exert control and conformity over the features used in production models. It allows data scientists to focus on solving problems rather than cleaning data and removes some of the problems in getting a model to production. It does, however, introduce coupling into the production system and can impede agility of data science innovation.

CHAPTER 20

Model Monitoring

Once your models have made it into production you cannot put your feet up and relax. You should, of course, celebrate that you have built something that has been deployed by a business. But to ensure that the success is not short lived you need to monitor how that model is performing as time goes on. There are several different facets to monitoring a data science solution, including many of the standard software monitoring tasks, such as:

1. How much is the system being used?
2. What resources is it consuming?
3. How often does it fail?
4. How are these statistics changing over time?

Each of these system monitoring tasks will help engineers manage and scale the deployment system to meet demand. However, machine learning models require additional forms of monitoring, because as described by data scientist Vishal Ramesh, machine learning models "can fail without making any noise."[1] Meaning that the system can flawlessly return results, but that the results are no longer reliable. There are a range of additional kinds of monitoring required to identify problems with a data science solution. These requirements fall into three categories:

1. The input data
2. The output data
3. The performance

---

[1] Ramesh, V. 2021. "Machine Learning Monitoring—What, Why, Where and How?" Blog Post, Towards Data Science. https://towardsdatascience.com/machine-learning-monitoring-what-why-where-and-how-873fa971afa8

Input Data

The model you have built and deployed as a solution, was created based on a specific data set. That data set had a range of properties that are in some sense embedded in your solution. It is generally implicit in any data science procedure that the data it is created with is representative of the data it will see in the future. Violation of this assumption can affect the performance of the model as well as the downstream systems such as the selection of thresholds and the design of any rules that act on the model predictions.

Most input data can be broken into a series of independent data points that can be monitored in the ways we will shortly explore. Some input data is inherently complex, such as the contents of free text fields. Complicated input data requires one of two approaches, you could develop a technique that is specific to that data, perhaps driven by what you know about how the data is being used in your model. Alternatively, if your modeling pipeline converts that data into a vector of independent features, then you can shift the monitoring to focus on the output of this processing step. In the vast majority of data science applications, the latter approach will be a sufficient method for model monitoring.

Once you have a set of independent numerical, Boolean and categorical variables, there are a range of different things that you can monitor about the data that the model receives over time. We outline them in the following subsections.

A. *Logical Rules*

Some data features will have business-specific definitions that do not permit certain values or preclude them from appearing in particular combinations with other features. For example, a service that is only sold and accessible to people over the age of 18, cannot have a customer record where either their age is less than 18 years, or the difference between their age and tenure is less than 18 years. This occurrence is contrary to the business policy.

Many business processes can be distilled into a set of logical rules that define conditions that must hold for a customer or product record. Violations of these logical rules can be taken as evidence that something has failed in the data collection or preparation pipeline.

B. Nulls

Some data features will have null values, either by being intrinsically unknown, or through unavoidable system errors. Typically, these nulls will be present in relatively constant ratios, even if they are not deterministic. You should monitor for any change in the distribution of null values across all fields. Changes in these distributions may indicate modifications, or failures, in the underlying systems. Even if the change involves a reduction in the number of nulls, it may mean that you should prepare to retrain the model as the data quality has improved.

C. Numerical Distributions

Any numerical data points will have some underlying distribution. You might represent this as a parametric distribution, or as a nonparametric distribution you capture in some quantized range of bins. You should monitor each numerical feature for changes in that distribution. You might monitor for significant changes in the mean, increases or decreases in the proportion of values lying at the extremes, or any other method of detecting distributional change, such as Kullback–Leibler Divergence.[2]

A widely used technique for monitoring changes in variable distributions for models is the population stability index (PSI). This is a metric calculated over two binned representations of distributions that can easily be applied to detect large changes in the distribution of both numeric and categorical data. It is a well-established technique for monitoring models in the finance industry.[3]

D. Categorical Distributions

Categorical variables also come with an underlying distribution that can change over time. You can apply simple monitoring of the mode of the

---

[2] S. Kullback, R.A. Leibler. 1951. "On Information and Sufficiency," *Annals of Mathematical Statistics* 22, no 1, pp. 79–86. doi:10.1214/aoms/1177729694

[3] B. Yurdakul. 2018. "Statistical Properties of Population Stability Index," *Dissertations*, 3208. https://scholarworks.wmich.edu/dissertations/3208

distribution, or the number of active categories. You can also apply PSI (discussed previously) to monitor changes in the overall distribution.

In many applications, it is important to monitor the number of new categories that are being presented to your model. Even if the modeling approach you use has an encoding method that transparently handles new values, the presence of new categories is often a strong indicator of fundamental changes in the underlying data generating process. If regular new values are expected in your business process, then attention should be shifted to the rate of new category emergence.

E. Anomalies and Outliers

In many real-world situations, the problems of input data start with minor effects that get worse over time. An early warning signal for a new and emerging problem can be the presence of a small number of strange or unusual records. For example, a new phone OS has just been released that causes problems for a model inside your application. Initial volumes of users are small, and you want to detect their problems and resolve the issue before there is widespread adoption of the new OS.

You can apply an anomaly detection algorithm to your training data, and then routinely apply it to your scoring data. In doing so, you are looking for records that are stranger than the most unusual training point. These outlier records could be your best early warning indicator of a looming problem.

Output Data

The solution you deliver will produce an output, whether it is a number, recommendation, or a multidimensional data structure. Whatever the output is, it will have an underlying distribution as well. You can baseline the solution using out-of-sample performance on your training data. This will allow you to monitor the solution for changes in its output distribution. All the techniques applied to monitoring your input data can be applied again to the output data.

In all likelihood, you will not see a change in the output distribution unless the input has changed. However, due to the nonlinear nature of

MODEL MONITORING   191

most machine learning models, it is possible that insignificant changes in the input generate large changes in the output. For example, tree-based models determine split points in numerical variables that determine which branch of the tree to follow. Thus, a small change in a variable used at the top of the tree can cause the output to be determined by an almost completely different part of the model.

In addition, monitoring the model output gives you greater transparency over potential business impacts. For example, if your churn rate is 0.1 percent of customers per month, then you do not want to see the model start increasing or decreasing the predicted proportion of churn. Either the model is being misled by a change in the input, or the effect is real, in which case you want to know about it.

Performance

The final aspect of data science monitoring is deterioration in the performance metrics you used to evaluate your solution. To do this you require the overall system architecture to provide feedback with data about the outcomes when they occur. For example, feeding back which customers churned, which products sold out, volumes of units sold, and so on.

For most data science solutions there will be a wide range of standard metrics that could be monitored. You should generally favor those metrics that are close to your method of ROI estimation. An ideal way to monitor the solution is through an ongoing estimation of financial impact. Such an approach would likely need some customization for each deployment, but it would provide very specific feedback to the business and would add urgency to any modifications that need to be made.

One difficulty with monitoring performance is that for many business problems you do not get the feedback signals until months or years have passed. If you are estimating customer lifetime value, or credit risk, or any long-term business outcome, then you need to wait until you have made the necessary observations to calculate performance changes.

As discussed in earlier chapters, having to wait long periods until events have occurred has necessitated the use of varying kinds of proxy signals. Model monitoring is no exception. One of the most used methods to mitigate this problem is to monitor the output distribution and flag any potential issues. The problem is: how do we know when drift in the output distribution is indicative of model decay?

One way of approaching this is to use your backtests to look for patterns in output drift that are indicative of problems. A simple example comes from fraud prediction. In most fraud problems you generally expect the nature of fraud to change over time; crime is a business like many others and criminals do not want to spend time on activity that does not pay (contrary to the common euphemism). This means that you should expect certain fraud activities to diminish over time as new forms of fraud emerge. For a model that has not been retrained you will expect that an increasing proportion of new fraud will start being missed.

How can we detect this in the output distribution?

When the kinds of fraud your model is trained to predict start to fall out of favor, then your model will be predicting that fewer events are fraudulent. If your model is saying that proportionally less fraud is being attempted you should not pat yourself on the back for a job well done (yet), you should be investigating to see if there is something happening that is missing. It may be that your model is sufficiently strong that you have dissuaded the fraudsters from attacking your systems, and hence the model is detecting fewer fraud attempts. If that is the case, then it is almost certain that they will have moved on to attack weaker targets in the market. Reach out through whatever industry contacts you have and try and find out where the fraud has moved.

Of course, some kinds of fraud are automated, in which case the volume of older, less-effective attacks will not necessarily diminish because there are low-cost methods to maintain the onslaught. In fact, there would be a pay-off for criminals in maintaining the onslaught of low-cost low-payoff fraud. Just like spam, it has a net positive benefit for the criminal. In addition, it also acts as a screen that helps disguise new and more subtle attacks. You are less likely to notice low-volume new attacks when your system is constantly propelling an onslaught of familiar attacks. An ideal monitoring system in this case would involve categorization of fraud attacks as automated or nonautomated, and monitor volumes and patterns of both.

The techniques described in this chapter can help spot shifting trends in the data and your model performance. The more you track, the more opportunities you will have to intervene. However, as the brief discussion of the complexities of fraud detection should indicate, there is no easy answer to the question of how best to monitor your solution. You will need to think about the process that generates your data, how it might change over time, and how you can detect potential problems.

Summary

Monitoring data science solutions requires a range of techniques, some from traditional software monitoring, and others that are specific to the field. In all instances, they are designed to detect issues with the data flowing in or out of your models. Ideally, you should focus your monitoring through an understanding of the processes that generate data as well as the potential financial impacts of different forms of change.

In the longer term, the information gained through model monitoring can be used to influence the data science process and the development of deployment architectures. An ideal end-to-end data science solution would include bespoke monitoring that is both sensitive to the specifics of your business, and able to initiate automated responses like data analysis or model retraining when problems are detected.

Conclusion

We have been through an end-to-end discussion of the process of doing data science. The focus has not been on specific algorithms, or statistical techniques; instead, we have examined the other details that affect the delivery of projects. This process began with framing the problem, collecting critical details, and communicating with stakeholders about what data science is and what it needs in order to succeed.

We covered the importance of deeply understanding how a data science project will impact the business and managing the client's expectations. We explored multiple standard types of data science project, and the common problems they face. We discussed the variety of people you will need to work with over the course of the project, and the challenges they can each bring. Working with people is a large part of being an effective data scientist. Very talented numerically minded people can sometimes struggle to carry a project through to a satisfied client because they can't manage the minutiae of getting stakeholders in agreement and keeping them there.

Finally, we discussed what is required to deliver your data science solutions such that they can be integrated with an organization's existing processes. These processes include technical and human considerations, as well as what we need to monitor in order to ensure that the solution will continue to deliver value long after it has been deployed.

Data scientists can sometimes struggle to remember that what matters to a business is getting results, not a perfect model. Simple models executed well and delivered quickly often bring more value than intricate, lovingly crafted models that take years to construct.

I would not be so bold as to claim that the principles in this book will ensure the success of your project. I do, however, assert that the collection of ideas and practices in this book have been distilled from many projects and conversations with experienced data scientists. Ultimately it is up to you to decide what makes sense and then experiment and see what appears to work. I hope you have found the book useful and practical for your career.

About the Author

John Hawkins is an Australian data scientist with a research background in machine learning for bioinformatics. He holds positions as the chief scientist for ad-tech company Playground XYZ, machine learning advisor for health-tech start-up HealthVox.org, and is an affiliate researcher with the Transitional AI Group at UNSW. He has 20 years of experience in solving problems in industry and academia, delivering data science solutions for organizations in software development, banking, insurance, media, ad-tech, and biomedical research. He holds a PhD in Computer Science from the University of Queensland, an associate degree in Information Technology from Southern Cross University, and a Bachelor of Arts (Honors I) in Philosophy from the University of Newcastle. He has written more than 20 peer-reviewed academic articles and presented at academic and industry conferences around the world. You can connect with him via his website: https://john-hawkins.github.io/

Index

www.ingramcontent.com/pod-product-compliance
Lightning Source LLC
Chambersburg PA
CBHW061213220326
41599CB00025B/4628